How can we stop racism in its tracks? What would it look like if heaven invaded earth? If those questions give you pause, this book is for you. My friend Ken Claytor has written a must-read for anyone desiring to be part of the solution to our world's race problem. Read this book and learn from one of the best.

—Stephen Chandler, Senior Pastor of Union Church

As It Is in Heaven is a book every person needs to read. It's easy to get lost in the endless debates about the existence (or non-existence) of racism. But our job as Christians is not to debate; our job is to lean in and extend love to our brothers and sisters who are hurting. We can't do that as long as we see our fellow image bearers as "other," and this book does a masterful job of reminding us that we are not "other"; we are one.

—Nona Jones, Business Executive, Pastor, Founder of Faith & Prejudice and best-selling Author, *Success from the Inside Out*

Ken's voice is one of racial reconciliation to this generation. In this book, you'll find an honest and encouraging conversation about loving all people regardless of their skin color. If you seek to understand God's heart about racism, without shame and degradation, this book is for you.

—Casey & Stacy Henagan, Pastors & Founders of KeyPoint Church

Joel Osteen and I count it an honor to have Ken and Tabatha as part of the Champion Network of Churches.

The journey this book takes you on is both inspiring and insightful. You'll laugh, cry, be disturbed, be surprised, feel the pain of racism… but above and beyond it all, you'll gain hope that racial reconciliation is possible. With empathy and not apathy, forgiveness and not divisiveness, faith and not fear—along with a deliberate commitment to "the process"— the human race can indeed live together on earth "As It Is in Heaven!" Brilliantly written and well researched, this book contains sixty-nine foot-notes and intriguing stories on nearly every page. It's scripturally sound and leaves no stone left unturned on such a crucial issue. This book will be a life changer.

Spoiler alert! After describing the problem from several perspectives, Ken offers the most convicting and convincing solution to this national crisis. You'll be transformed and thankful that you read this book, and so will everyone else!

—Phil Munsey, Chairman of Champions Network of Churches of Lakewood Church/Joel Osteen Ministries

As It Is in Heaven is a much-needed book for the times in which we are living. My friend Ken Claytor addresses the most important question:

How does God view race, and how does that impact the way we view race—which then impacts how we respond to the racial issues of our day. This book a must-read for all people.

—Benny Perez, Lead Pastor of ChurchLV

Ken Claytor is an incredible leader and a valuable voice for this generation. In the midst of a divided nation in turmoil, he offers a much-needed remedy, not only bringing unity but hope.

When most people just sit back and point out the problem, Ken Claytor has sat down to pen out the solution. This will be a great resource for years to come.

—Shaun Nepstad, Lead Pastor of Fellowship Church and Author of *Don't Quit in the Dip*

With a sincere and vulnerable heart, Ken graciously approaches the topic of racial unrest that has divided humans for far too long. By asking the simple question, "How does God view race?" Ken takes readers on a journey of the heart and challenges us to drop our views, ideas, and opinions and pick up God's perspective. Regardless of our skin color, culture, or past experiences, Ken encourages us all to be a part of the solution by putting Jesus at the center. This book will make you uncomfortable in the best way possible and challenge you to love others here on earth as it is in heaven.

—Randy Bezet, Lead Pastor of Bayside Community Church

As It Is in Heaven has identified the race problem as an issue of love. I was moved by the personal accounts and insights from Pastor Ken's life. I quickly related and reflected on how similar situations in my past have influenced my thinking patterns as a son, husband, and professional athlete. Everyone should read this powerful book and discover how alike we actually are. We are all imperfect people serving a perfect God. Amid the social unrest, this book concentrates on the solution.

—Christian Taylor, two-time Olympic Champion

When the world is telling us to think one way, the Bible shows us another way to think and live regarding race. *As It Is in Heaven* by Ken Claytor is a must-read. He pairs the practical with deep insights into scripture and shows us that we can live like heaven on earth with all people.

His life reflects this message, and he lives what he teaches in live a Christlike, unifying life.

Ken Claytor is a husband, father, friend and strong man. His wisdom and perspective help us all see through God's eyes rather than through the darkness of division and anger. *As It Is in Heaven* will encourage and empower you to reach a new level of human understanding and compassion.

—Casey Treat, Senior Pastor of Christian Faith

As It Is in Heaven is a powerful teaching that reveals God's heart for His Church! I highly recommend this book for anyone wanting to dig deeper into the power of unity within God's church and Satan's plan to steal, kill, and destroy. Pastor Ken does a phenomenal job of bringing to life the adversity we face as the Church, but also how we overcome as one body! What we go through should drive us to fight with one another rather than against one another. God's will has always been for His Church to come together—regardless of race, background, theological beliefs, or economic status—because we can accomplish far more together. This book will ignite you to walk in your appointed authority and play your part in increasing God's kingdom.

—Pastor Mike & Dr. Dee Dee Freeman, Pastors and
Founders of Spirit of Faith Christian Center

The true mark of a Christian is our desire to be peacemakers. Because of this, there has been a deliberate assault on unity. Regardless of our backgrounds, we are stronger together and all of hell knows that. The snare of racism is not new, but is evident even in the book of Genesis.

In response, Ken offers a must-read, refreshing guide on how to deal with the racial issues of our day. *As It Is in Heaven* offers us a fresh perspective on racism, pushing us towards a loving and empathetic approach that looks to see things God's way and lean on Him to find the solutions.

Ken, through his sincerity and vulnerability, takes us on a journey to figure out how God views race, and how we can find hope and unity in the midst of a society that seems so divided at times. You'll laugh, you'll cry, and most importantly, I believe you'll find hope, forgiveness, and a kingdom perspective.

—Travis Greene, Lead Pastor and six-time
Grammy-Nominated Worship Artist

Pastor Ken and Tabatha's genuine love, inspiring leadership, and courageous faith combine to leave an indelible impact on the communities they serve and the people they lead. Far too often, Christian leaders intellectually affirm the biblical mandate for unity without ever aggressively pursuing it. As It Is in Heaven builds a compelling biblical case for unity in our diversity and further illustrates how it can practically transpire through Pastor Ken's personal, intentional journey. I'm thankful for his friendship and example and this timely and valuable resource.

—Dominic Russo, Founder of Missions.Me & Love Has No Limits

Cover design by: Sara Young
Cover photo by: Andrew van Tilborgh

ISBN: 978-1-954089-94-5   1 2 3 4 5 6 7 8 9 10

Printed in the United States of America

AS IT IS IN
HEAVEN

────────────── ○ ──────────────

HOW A CHURCH THAT RESEMBLES HEAVEN
CAN HELP HEAL OUR RACIAL DIVIDE

KEN CLAYTOR

AVAIL

Dedication

I dedicate this book to my mom and dad, Barbara and C. W. Claytor. Thank you for teaching me that I could be anything I wanted to be. Thank you for allowing me to dream without limits. Thank you for not passing down to me racist ideologies and stereotypical perspectives. Thank you for helping me see early on that people are people and that we have all been made in the image and likeness of God. I honor you, look up to you, and love you both more than you could ever know.

CONTENTS

ACKNOWLEDGMENTS

To my Alive Church family: You guys are amazing. Without you, this book would not be a reality. I would still be scratching my head somewhere, wondering, *Why can't we all get along?* Thank you for journeying with me over the past decade and not giving up on the fight.

For our church to resemble heaven, you all have had to put certain things on the altar. Some of you have sacrificed your favorite music, the style of church that you are accustomed to, your past traditions, and your own personal expectations and hopes. We have laughed and cried together as we have tried to figure this whole thing out. Some things worked and some things, well, not that much.

Hopefully, when you look up and see the diversity in our church, so many different cultures and classes of people worshiping together as family, you are proud of what we have built. Not with an ungodly pride, but a proper sense of accomplishment: this has been God's doing, and we have all been a part of a modern-day miracle.

Thank you for praying for me and my family and for trusting the God in me to bring this vision to pass. It means more than the world. Also, thank you for being bridge builders and for being intentional in your love. Thank you for not being exclusive but for being inclusive. Thank you for making room for people. Thank you for changing lives.

To Tabatha, my wife and best friend of twenty-two years: Wow! Time flies when you are having fun. I have never in my life met anyone like you. I am amazed by your grace, your style, your swag, your kingdom perspective, and your understanding of spiritual truths. You are my good thang and my favor from the Lord. You embody one race—you are so white at times, so black at other times. You break the box. I love it! Thank you for living this message out with me. Thank you for fighting with me to see people like God does, as one race: the human race.

To my children: Hannah, Charity, and Kenny. You all are my heart. Each one of you is gifted and special in your own way. Thank you for allowing me to be up late at night, up early in the morning, to travel here and there, and to still be a father to you. You are intelligent, valuable, and capable, and God is going to use you each in a unique way. I am honored to be your father. I will allow you to marry anyone you want to—as long as they love Jesus, love you, and are not called Chewbacca (haha!).

To Casey and Stacy Henagan, thank you for encouraging me to press on to complete this project. To Andy Butcher, Wendy Jenkins, Sheri Still, and Samantha Wright, thank you for all of your support and efforts!

And to Jesus, the Lord of my life: I just want to hear you say, "Well done."

Ken Claytor

Orlando, Florida

INTRODUCTION

THE HUMAN RACE

A s you open this book, my prayer is that you will begin to see the heavenly perspective and insight that God has so graciously gifted—that no matter the date or time you read this, whether our countries are in the midst of turmoil or experiencing a span of reprieve, the overarching themes you walk away with are love, unity, and reconciliation. Aside from love, unity is the most powerful weapon the Christian church holds in its hearts and hands. In order for reconciliation to take place, for His kingdom to come, unity with one another is what is needed—desperately.

America continues to experience rampant racial tensions that have been ongoing in our country for hundreds of years. These tensions ebb and flow and may never be relieved until our Savior returns, but for the Christian, whether you live in America, Israel, Africa, or China, you war with mixed emotions as you hear news of deaths and protests and the political debates and fallouts that have followed. You may feel righteous anger at the injustice, concern over the destruction, and apprehension—perhaps even a reticent despair—for the future. The world's racial wounds seem as deep and as ugly as ever. Is there really any hope?

The answer is yes, absolutely—but only if we answer the most fundamental question. It's not how to right past wrongs, or what needs to be done to ensure justice and equal opportunities for all, as important as those issues are. The million-dollar question is this: "How does God view race?" Because only when we get His perspective are we going to find lasting solutions.

The surprising thing is that God is less concerned about race than we are! Now, don't get me wrong. I'm not saying He is disinterested in prejudice. Nor am I saying that the color of our skin is unimportant to Him. He created us all equally in His image, choosing different colors to reflect some of His amazing diversity. As that old children's song goes, "Red, brown, yellow, black, and white, they are precious in His sight."[1] God chose your color for you, and it is beautiful!

That is not what is most important to Him. We may focus on the externals—what others look like—but God doesn't. He made that clear when He sent the prophet Samuel to find a new king for Israel. God told him to ignore the widely-accepted candidates, Jesse's older sons. "The Lord does not look at the things people look at. People look at the outward appearance, but the Lord looks at the heart," he said in 1 Samuel 16:7.

God simply doesn't recognize racial differences the way we do today. In fact, of the 730,000 or so words in the Bible (depending on which translation you use), in the King James Version, there is no mention of the word "race" the way we use it today. When God speaks of people, He does so in terms of nationalities and people groups: Jews and Gentiles, saved and unsaved. When God looks at us, He sees only one *race*—the human race.

---

1   C. Herbert Woolston, "Jesus Loves the Little Children," *Hymntime*, http://www.hymntime.com/tch/htm/j/e/s/l/jesloves.htm.

Sadly, some of us have been duped into majoring on a minor. We have allowed a distinction God does not make to divide us. Like boxers, we have retreated to our corners. They fight for the color of their corner, red or blue, while we fight for the color of our skin, whether that's black, brown, red, white, or some other color. When the bell rings, we come out swinging! This just does not have to be.

FIGHTING TOGETHER

Instead of punching each other, we should be coming together to fight our common enemy. At the end of the day, racism is not a social or a cultural issue; it is a sin issue, and there is ultimately only one answer to sin: the risen Jesus. That is why while activists, business leaders, community organizers, educators, police, politicians, and protesters all have a part to play in healing our racial divide, they're not where our greatest hope lies.

I believe that the single most important role falls to followers of Jesus. We have to show that there is a better way. What is that? Well, when Jesus taught His first disciples what we now call the Lord's Prayer, He prayed, "Your kingdom come, your will be done, *on earth as it is in heaven*" (Matthew 6:10, emphasis added).

The glimpses we get of heaven in Scripture reveal a group of people not separated by their different colors but united by their shared commitment to and worship of Jesus as the hope and Savior of the world. This is one of the main kingdom components that God gifts us with through His holy Word: a church that resembles heaven is filled with individuals who value diversity and who are united in their pursuit of Him. It is why I have committed myself to leading an intentionally multiracial, multiethnic church over the past decade. Please remember, the church is not some organization or building, so when I use the term "the church," I'm speaking directly about you and me, individual members who are born-again believers. We make up the body, and we ARE the church.

Of course, there are big social issues—like inequality and injustice—to resolve when it comes to racism. However, all the laws and all the programs in the world won't be enough without a change of heart—in you and in me.

I have been working on this message over the last ten years or so in response to events that took place thousands of years ago when sin entered the world in the Garden of Eden. While the racial unrest of more recent times has saddened me, it has also renewed and re-energized my commitment to being part of the answer by helping establish God's kingdom here "as it is in heaven." As things stand, we are a long, long way from seeing that happen. Sadly, the body of Christ is not unified in the way that it needs to be for God to be able to pour out His full blessing on us.

As a pastor, my passion is to see men, women, and children of all ethnicities finding their true identities in God and being transformed into all that He has planned for them to be—together. Only in that way will we be able to reflect the real richness of who God is to a world that so desperately needs to hear the good news of Jesus Christ.

I know that my perspective won't be exactly the same as a black person who endured being hosed down, jailed, or beaten in the 1960s while marching in support of civil rights, or a white person born in the rural Midwest who may never have been in community with a person of color. My book—my message—is not intended to be offensive, though it could be challenging to some. Rather, it is an invitation to journey along the road of self-reflection that promotes God's gracious healing and a personal commitment to being part of the solution.

We are never going to end racism once and for all this side of heaven because we live in a broken world with a lot of broken people. However, we can for sure give it a really good punch in the mouth! We can make a big difference. We can heal some of racism's wounds, repair some of its damage, bridge some of its divides, and prevent some of its spread.

I don't believe you are reading this by accident. As a matter of fact, my team and I have been praying that this book would find its way into the hands of people around the world whom God is calling to be part of the solution, not the problem. My hope is that it will help equip you, your local church body, and your family with some of the perspectives and principles that are needed to bring further healing—in our nation, in our churches, and mostly in our own hearts towards our fellow human beings.

I hope that, in the following pages, you catch something of the vision for the kind of church that I believe most fully demonstrates God's heart to humankind—the kind of church that is the answer to the world's racial problem. A church that knows only one race—the human race.

CHAPTER ONE

SEEING COLOR FOR THE FIRST TIME

I f you ever want to get a lump in your throat, go online and check out the video of two color-blind brothers getting to put on a pair of corrective glasses for the first time.[2] Make sure you have a box of tissues close at hand, because you could sniffle a bit.

The boys are just two of millions of people who don't see vibrant colors like the rest of us do. Their visual palette is dulled and muted. Now, though, people can get special lenses that adjust the way their eyes take in the light, increasing the brightness of different colors to match the way others experience them.

It's so moving to watch these people react to seeing in full color for the first time in their lives as they are presented with a pair of these remarkable glasses. They stare up at the sky in amazement, they look down at their clothes in wonder, they gape in awe at the different-colored balloons often

---

2 "Colorblind brothers overwhelmed by seeing color for the first time," *YouTube*, June 21, 2016, https://www.youtube.com/watch?v=m1X0QTTtPmc.

presented with their gift-wrapped glasses. And they weep with joy as they see the world differently—in all its beautiful color.

My awakening to the way other people see color wasn't so heartwarming. Instead of tears of happiness shared with others, it provoked tears of hurt and anger that I choked down so no one could see them.

It happened when I was around thirteen years old, sitting in class at Park Junior High School in Beckley, West Virginia. This was back in the early nineties before color-correcting glasses had been developed. What changed the way I saw the world was not lenses but a folded-up piece of paper.

It started with a girl. Let's call her Tiffany. She was sitting at the desk in front of me as we waited for the next lesson to start. She turned to me and passed a note, motioning for me to pass it on to someone sitting a few rows behind me. This was standard junior high practice before the days of texting—you shared messages across the room hand to hand, hopefully without the teacher spotting you.

The unspoken rule was that you didn't look. You just passed the note on to the next person in line and made sure they knew where it was supposed to go. I was a bit of a mischievous kid at times, so I remember one occasion when I ignored the note "honor code" and peeked at one that I was helping make its way to a friend of mine. The note was from his girlfriend, and in it she called him Pooh Bear. Poor guy; I didn't let him live that down for some time.

That move was out of the ordinary, though, so to this day I don't know what possessed me to unfold Tiffany's note. I had no reason to suspect her of anything negative or nasty. To me, she was just one of the girls in some of my classes—nice enough, even if I didn't know her very well. Oh, and she was white, but that didn't really register as important. Yet.

It took a moment or two for what I was seeing to sink in. Because it was such a defining moment, you might expect that I could quote what was written verbatim, like the words were burned into me. But for some reason—maybe the grace of God—I can't. All I can remember is seeing swastika symbols and words like "white power" and "KKK" (meaning Ku Klux Klan—an American white supremacist hate group) and the shock and the hurt and the anger. The takeaway was unmistakable: black was inferior.

I looked at Tiffany in disbelief. "What in the world is this?"

That classroom explosion rippled throughout the school. For a time, it seemed like some kind of teenage race war might break out. Parents and staff weighed in to try to calm things down. Kids on both sides of the "aisle," so to speak, were grappling with their own emotional responses as well as how and where payback and vengeance might be served, growing their own deep-seated grudges. Poor Tiffany had made some real enemies. Fortunately for her, I guess, Tiffany was transferred to another school within a matter of days.

The incident blew over in time, as junior high dramas will, but something had changed for me forever. For the first time in my life, I was aware that people looked at me differently—looked down on me—because of the color of my skin. Now, I knew that racism existed, of course. But it had always been something that was "out there" somewhere, not really part of my everyday world.

By opening Tiffany's note, I had learned that some people see colors differently than others. Not in a beautiful way, like with those corrective glasses, but in an ugly one. And though I couldn't have articulated it clearly if you had asked me back then, beneath the pain was something else—a conviction that this just wasn't right, and I wanted, somehow, to be a part of changing things for the better one day.

HERITAGE

I came into the world on May 4, 1978, in a small town in southern West Virginia, which has recently been named the most racist state in the country. The regrettable ranking was based on an analysis of millions of tweets posted between 2014 and 2016 and those containing racial slurs.[3]

West Virginia may have come into being in 1861 after breaking away from Virginia to side with the Union North after the start of the Civil War, but a casual visitor today might be surprised at the prevalence of Confederate flags across the state. The "most racist" tag may be disputable, but there's no question that race is and has been an issue there.

I was mostly unaware of its prevalence until my Park Junior High School awakening. I credit that innocence largely to the way my parents raised my younger sister and me. They taught us to be proud of who we were and to hold our heads up high, but not to look down on anyone else for who they were. Honoring our heritage didn't mean we had to hate other people.

When I was born, my parents lived on a dirt road in a two-bedroom mobile home in the Red Brush area, one of Beckley's predominantly lower-income neighborhoods. Both young educators, Mom and Dad may not have been high earners; however, they were hard workers willing to pay their dues like everyone else. Over time, they met their goals and were able to move us to a home in a better part of town. Beckley is not known for being highly diverse—per the most recent census data, the demographics of the city are currently: 72.6 percent white, 21.4 percent black, 2.0 percent Asian, 2.7 percent two or more races, and 1.2 percent Hispanic or Latino.

During my childhood years, churches were still largely segregated due to many factors but primarily location. The church we attended was all black but for one interracial couple. The ratio at my school, Lincoln Elementary, was different—more of a mix to be sure. Even this, however,

---

3 "Most Racist States 2020," *WorldPopulationReview*, https://worldpopulationreview.com/states/most-racist-states/.

did not inhibit my first encounter with teasing and discrimination from other kids. This had nothing to do with my color though. Both my parents taught there at the time, so that made me a bit unpopular with some of the students. You know, teacher's pet and all that.

One of the games we played in elementary school involved passing around a piece of paper on which you had to write down the names of the two girls you thought were the cutest in the class. I know most of you remember that "check the box" note being passed around class. For me, one girl was black and the other white. It wasn't about equal opportunities; it was just the way I saw them. I made my evaluations on their hair, their eyes, their faces, their smiles, and their personalities.

Growing up, some of my closest friends were white. I'd hang out with Shaun and Jeremy all the time, none of us ever thinking about the color difference, as far as I was aware. I'd have sleepovers with them. At Jeremy's, we would spend hours bouncing on the trampoline in his back yard. His mom had her own business, and she would help sponsor our basketball team.

At home, we didn't ignore race, but we didn't major on it either. I never heard either of my parents talk negatively about others. I believe this was due to them having interactions with all kinds of people in their day-to-day lives. As a sports coach, Dad loved to play tennis, in which he was surely the minority; but that never phased him, and he made many great friends due to this exposure.

While neither Mom nor Dad were militant about being black, they made sure that we were aware of our heritage and history—Mom especially. She really is our family historian and even began our family reunion which has been happening for the past forty years. She made a point of celebrating Black History Month every year. She would tell us all about some of our black pioneers—people like Harriet Tubman, Jackie Robinson, Rosa Parks, and, of course, Dr. Martin Luther King Jr. She also tried to incorporate the Kwanzaa celebration, originally intended to be a sort of alternative to

Christmas, which centers on black culture. She'd wear African colors as part of the celebrations, but it was something that never really captured my interest or imagination—I was still at an age where I was more into the traditional Christmas and getting wrapped presents under the tree than learning about culture. And my biggest boyhood hero was Michael Jordan. In him, I saw someone to aspire to be on the basketball court.

All the things from our heritage my mother exposed us to came from a place of goodness and the standpoint of a good educator wanting her students to know their full story. Even though she wanted me to know where I had come from, she never forced these lessons on me with bitterness, anger, or malice.

One of the biggest influences on me when I was growing up in regards to my heritage didn't come from Mom's curriculum. It came from television. I couldn't wait for Thursday nights so I could tune into *The Cosby Show*. I'd watch that and its spin-off, *Different World*, back-to-back.

We are all aware that Bill Cosby's portrayal of the upstanding Dr. Huxtable couldn't stand up to what occurred in his real day-to-day life—that is the reality of most sitcoms/television shows. I do not debate one bit the wrongness of what he has been accused of, but there is no way around how significant that program was to me and many other young minority people. Most minority actors and actresses on television or in the movies back then seemed to be cast as villains or gangsters of one kind or another.

And whenever a member of the black community was interviewed on the television news, it always appeared to me like the producers went out of their way to select the most inarticulate representative they could. Meanwhile, in Cosby's Cliff Huxtable character, we saw a successful man—a doctor with an attorney wife and a loving family. It showed me that being successful was not limited to one race. It was open and available to anyone who would work hard and chase the "dream." It gave me and many other young black children something very concrete to aspire to.

As a result of this and my parents' example, I don't recall ever being aware of a gulf between whites, blacks, yellows, browns, and reds. If my parents did try to make it clear to me when I was young, in any way, it's like God must have covered my ears. Sure, I knew that there were differences—that Shaun and Jeremy weren't just like me—but those differences simply didn't matter.

And then Tiffany passed me her note. I don't know how much she really believed what she had written—and, if she did mean it, whether that was all she had been raised to know. Maybe she was just looking for a way to fit in with others; junior high school is a bit like the Wild West: a time for exploring new frontiers that hide all kinds of dangers. Throw in some raging hormones, and you've got an explosion waiting to happen.

Adolescence is a season when kids start to seriously separate into different tribes. They begin to develop their own identities and try out different ones like new clothes. The sad thing is that, for many teenagers, "becoming their own person" actually means trying to fit in with a particular group and adopting its ways and values, even when those values clash with what they have been raised to know. Peer pressure and the desire to be accepted can make vulnerable young people cruel to others.

Outwardly, I blew the Tiffany thing off, but inside I was hurting. I just didn't understand why people could have a problem with me because of the color of my skin. It made no sense to me whatsoever; but try as I might, I couldn't shake it off. Then, a couple more things happened to hammer home the point that, whether I liked it or not, color was a problem to a whole lot of people out there.

Not long after I busted Tiffany for her note, I went on a ski trip to Winterplace Ski Resort in Ghent, West Virginia, about a twenty-minute drive from home. At that time, if black people stood out on the tennis courts because they were in the minority, then they were even more conspicuous on the slopes—and not just because of all the contrasting snow! I'd been introduced to the sport by a friend of the family, the fabulous smooth jazz musician Marion Meadows, and fallen in love with it.

I'd gone to Winterplace with Jeremy and a couple of other guys. At the top of one of the runs, we came across some other kids from school, including this one huge white guy. He must have been 6' 6" at least, and in all his ski gear, he seemed almost as wide. As we stood around, he made it clear that he didn't think black people should be allowed up on the mountain. He casually used the n-word as he made his point: I didn't belong.

I was about as mad as I had ever been. We went back and forth some, and I said we should take our skis off, go down to the parking lot and have this thing out. At some point, I realized that his size outweighed my indignation, and I could tell that Jeremy was scared—he'd gone quiet, kind of caught between wanting to stand up for me and fearing the big guy. I managed to scale back the confrontation, but I was left feeling really angry.

Superstition says that bad things come in threes, and it was the next incident that finally made me keenly aware of the racial divide surrounding me. This incident really broke my heart, and I can look back and see that this is where my heart, as a young man, began to harden.

Let's just call her Sarah. She was the cutest girl to me. We met in band, where I played the snare drum and she played the flute. I'd never been shy about talking to girls, unlike some of my friends, and we soon struck up a friendship. We'd talk all the time at practices and events, and pretty soon, it was major puppy love. We sat together whenever there were band outings, and we passed notes in school. There was nothing physical—we were only fourteen—but I liked her a lot.

Wannabe "player" that I was, I decided to go one better than a handwritten note. I borrowed a camcorder and videoed myself dancing to a Bobby Brown song, lip-syncing the words and performing all the latest popular dance moves. I'm embarrassed to even think about it today!

As you might suspect, my dance video fell into the wrong hands—her father's. But he wasn't just mad that some kid was spitting game to his teenage daughter—it's that I was black. He told Sarah in no uncertain terms that she couldn't have anything to do with me. Then he went down to the school and announced that he wanted the teachers to call him if they saw me hanging out with her. He said he would pull her out of school, if necessary, to keep us apart.

One of the band instructors took me aside one day. She tried to downplay the racial thing as she gently warned me that I might want to back off to avoid causing a scene. Sarah was really scared by it all. We tried to find ways and places to talk without being caught, but it was too much pressure, and our young love fizzled out.

I was left heartbroken. And angry. It just didn't make any sense to me. I was generally a pretty good kid. I was an honor roll student, the son of respected educators/teachers, respectful, etc., but I wasn't good enough to date this guy's daughter solely because I was black.

There was nowhere for me to take all my feelings. My parents were kind, caring, and loving, but we didn't have a history of deep conversations about emotions and that sort of thing. Plus, how many fourteen-year-old boys are going to tell their parents that they are in love with a girl and that their heart is broken? Not many.

All of this led to a gradual, quiet distancing that I wasn't really aware of at the time. If you had asked me, I wouldn't have said that I had a thing against white people. I'd tell you that I had come to recognize that some of them had a thing against me, but that was their problem—not mine.

However, a subtle racial rift was developing. I began to drift away. My old friendships with Jeremy and Shaun faded naturally. When I was with my friends, we'd sometimes joke around and act like some of the kids we knew, saying "White power" and "Heil Hitler!" We were overcompensating, trying to take the sting out of it all by laughing at it. I also found myself sometimes saying things like, "White people this," or, "White people that"—generalizations I had never made before.

Around this time, the Rodney King episode exploded. People across the nation were incensed by the violent beating of King by four Los Angeles Police Department officers. I was aware of the level of outrage, but it still seemed a bit distant to me.

I finally realized something had shifted in me when I reached my senior year and started dating a young lady who was both kind and intelligent—and who also happened to be white. While I really liked her, part of me was somehow embarrassed at the same time. I only recognized this when she would ask to hold my hand in public and I would refuse because I didn't want other people to know we were going together. I wasn't necessarily bothered about what whites would think of me, but I was concerned what some of my black friends might say. Part of me felt like I was letting the team down, somehow, while the rest of me resisted the idea that color needed to be some kind of dividing line.

I wouldn't be able to settle these inner tugs-of-war until I discovered that this race issue wasn't just something I had to sort out in my head. I also had to resolve it in my heart.

CHAPTER TWO

A GLIMPSE OF HEAVEN

I'd like to tell you that my journey toward racial unity was born out of an intense hunger to see God's kingdom expressed on earth as it is in heaven. But to be honest, it all started with my appetite for cake. Your birthday, my birthday, Christmas, someone graduated or had a baby, it didn't matter—I'd have a slice of whatever was on offer, to celebrate. The bigger the better.

I've gotten a bit more health-conscious over the years, so I am more careful about what I eat these days; but it was the gift of cake that got me to a midweek church meeting in Temple Hills, Maryland, in the fall of 2001. Tabatha and I had moved to the area the previous year after graduating from West Virginia University. We were newlyweds up to our ears in school and six figures of debt—if you're wondering—and determined to make it in the Washington, D.C., area.

It was hard going to begin with. Tabatha's first job was selling postage machines commercially, door-to-door. I started out helping a friend with his painting business for a couple hundred dollars here and there while I worked out how best to apply my business management degree.

Through a friend, Tabatha got a job as an executive assistant that paid better than her sales gig and also saved her from having to hustle around to calls by bus (we had only one car). The relative financial security allowed me to go into real estate. The guaranteed income was less than some other opportunities I had, but the prospects were greater. I had some confidence that I could do okay, and I also knew that we needed to earn some serious money to make a dent in what we owed.

I understood there wouldn't be overnight success, but we continued to struggle for what seemed like ages as I learned all I could about the real estate world. Things finally seemed to be looking up when I scored three deals that were due to bring me $26,000 in commission. But they closed just as I was leaving one company for another, and the owner kept the money that was due to me.

So we were struggling, working hard during the day and coming home in the evenings to a one-bedroom apartment with roaches and mice.

Enter this kind couple to whom I'd been showing some different properties. They hadn't made an offer on anything, but they were nice, and they seemed to like me. When they gave me a cake as a token of appreciation for my efforts, I was grateful, and when they then invited me to a Tuesday night thing at the church they attended, I thought, *Why not?*

I didn't mind a bit of religion. I'd grown up in church. We'd been regulars at Beckley's New Hope Baptist Church, where Dad drove the church van and cared for the elderly. Even though I had been raised in church and the message had gotten in, like most teenagers and young adults, I had not yet surrendered to living for God. My sister and I attended the church functions, Vacation Bible School and all of that, and my parents' lessons through biblical principles certainly shined through my sister and me, since we were taught to always be honest, kind, and respectful. But as far as living out my faith day to day, that wasn't me.

I was never a bad kid, but I was mischievous. I knew to keep my transgressions within limits. I'd kind of creep right up to the red line and wave a foot in the air over it without ever quite crossing it. As a result, I never got suspended from school, but I sure fidgeted through my share of Saturday detentions.

Maybe that all had something to do with my getting saved when I was eleven years old. Our church was kind of old school, and the pastor would put out a chair and invite anyone who wanted to receive Jesus to come forward to it. "Will there be one?" he would ask. Normally there wasn't, but this one Sunday, I went up to the front of the church. I knew when I sat down in that chair that I was stepping toward Jesus in some way, but I didn't really understand all that was going on. No one ever explained salvation to me, or what it meant to give your life to Jesus, even when I was baptized in water a few weeks later.

Thankfully, God kept His side of the agreement even if I did not truly understand or honor mine. I believed in Him—but in the same kind of abstract way that I had for a long time believed in racism—it was something that was planted, but I had not yet surrendered to living it out for myself. As a result, for the next ten years or so I lived as what Pastor Craig Groeschel calls a Christian atheist—I believed in Jesus but lived like He didn't exist.

I had a Bible, but I never cracked it open. I'd talk about God sometimes, when it seemed appropriate, and I even went to church once in a while. As I got older, the disconnect between what I believed and the way I behaved grew wider. I'd always been confident and outgoing, and I was a pretty good dancer. I rapped a little bit, too—one time, I won a freestyle rap contest on an MTV Spring Break trip. I loved a good party.

I never did drugs, but I could drink with the best of them, and I did. We'd hold parties with a trash container full of jungle juice—a rough mix of one hundred proof grain alcohol and Kool-Aid—and get hold of a tank of nitrous oxide used for inflating balloons and let people take hits from it to get high. Clearly, if you had put me in a police lineup with ten of my closest non-Christian friends, you wouldn't have been able to single me out as any different, unless maybe we were asked to speak: I didn't swear. Perhaps it was because I had never heard my parents use profanity when I was a kid. This was just standard life operation for me—I never felt the need to use profanity, so all my friends knew that I had a big thing about not cussing.

You could have driven a truck through the gap between what I held to be true and how I actually lived, especially as I left home and went off to school; and I tried to narrow this gap in some ways. I came up with my own religious practices. For instance, because Sunday was the Sabbath, a holy day, I wouldn't listen to any of the music I normally listened to, which was filled with perversion, murder, and mayhem. But at midnight on Monday, I'd crank it right back up again without a concern. On Sundays, I'd go to church if I could—which meant if I got up in time. If I didn't make it, I would "do something for God" instead, like go down the street from where I lived to the chapel located in the university hospital, where I would get down on one knee and say a quick prayer.

One thing I did know from my younger days in church was that the Bible said God would forgive us our sins if we said we were sorry. I became a professional confessor! I would tell God I was sorry for the things I had done that didn't please Him, ask for forgiveness, and figure everything was cool between us. Then I went right back to all that I had been doing. Somewhere along the way, I had missed the lesson about true repentance involving a change of heart and a change of ways.

With all that churchy background, I wasn't too uncomfortable about meeting my cake-giving clients at the church they were part of in Temple Mills. Things there were very different to what I was used to, however.

First off, they were meeting in a big old building that dwarfed the church I had grown up in. As first-timers, Tabatha and I were given VIP visitor badges and a warm welcome. Inside, the crowd was amazing. There must have been almost a couple thousand people there—on a weeknight. Very different from what I had been used to. There was great music for worship, really off the hook! The songs were nothing like the traditional ones I was familiar with. All in all, I was having a pretty good time.

When the guest preacher asked who wanted to give $1,000 to the Lord, I was all in. I took Tabatha's hand and tugged her to stand up with me. I wasn't trying to fit in or show off; I just wanted to be part of what was going on. I'd always tried to be generous whenever I did go to church. Where most of my friends might throw in a dollar bill or two when the collection came around, I'd usually make it a twenty, even if I didn't have much money. It just felt like the right thing to do. Maybe I figured it would help cover for some of my indiscretions.

Now, a thousand dollars was a whole other level of generosity, especially with the financial situation Tabatha and I were in. But I didn't care. The speaker told everyone who'd responded to his appeal to come down to the front of the church to be prayed for, so Tabatha and I got out of our seats and joined about a dozen or so people down there. Only then did I realize we were supposed to give the money that night. I'd thought it was more of a future pledge. I gave all that I had on me, a couple hundred bucks, while promising myself to make up the difference sometime.

Then the speaker began to pray for people, putting his hand on their foreheads. This was different from my Baptist boyhood, too. When they started to fall down on the floor as he prayed for them, it got even stranger. *There's no way I am doing that,* I said to myself as I waited our turn to be prayed for.

Taking a firm grasp of Tabatha's hand, I planted my feet squarely. The speaker put his hand on Tabatha's forehead. The next thing I knew she was falling and, from the presence and power of God I felt through her, I was falling too. I landed on my back and lay there unmoving for maybe thirty seconds or so. This incredible peace had settled over me like a blanket, warm and comforting and at the same time so heavy I could not move. *I don't believe this is happening*, I thought.

Then it passed, and I sat up, unsure for a moment where I was. Oh, yes—in a church, believe it or not. I had no idea what had happened as Tabatha and I made our way back to our seats, but I knew that I wanted to find out more—and that we would be back the next Sunday.

UNLEARNING OUR OLD WAYS

I'd gone to church because I'd been grateful for cake, but I came away with something much greater—a taste of what being a Christian really meant. It wasn't just about going to church and obeying the rules. It was about an encounter with a living God who wasn't locked up in a book of old stories—He was alive and present.

Now Tabatha and I had a whole new appetite. We couldn't get enough. We would be at church every chance we could get. Like sponges, we wanted to soak up everything that was available—and to share what we had found with others. We'd invite everyone along with us. When the time came for regulars to introduce any guests they had brought with them, we would often have to signal to a whole row of folks to stand up and be greeted.

Life started to turn around pretty quickly. Within three months of beginning to attend this lively church regularly, Tabatha was healed of chronic depression that had hung over her like a dark cloud for twelve years. You wouldn't have known it about her from casual acquaintance because she always put on a brave face to the world, but she lived under a heavy cloud for a long time.

The roots went back to her childhood. She was raised in an interracial home with a black father and a white mother. She felt caught between the two worlds growing up in Uniontown, Pennsylvania. She wasn't dark enough for her black friends, but she wasn't light enough for her white friends either. She got called all kinds of names. As if that wasn't enough, she also lost her father when she was just six years old. He wasn't there to provide for her or to protect her. These were hard times for them—emotionally, financially, and physically.

Tabatha's depression wasn't the only thing that God healed as we got involved in the church. He also rescued our marriage. We had been crazy in love when we first met and got married in my old childhood church back in Beckley, but we were young, and I, for one, was foolish. Plus, we were being crushed by the debt we owed and didn't know how to rise spiritually above our physical circumstances. If we weren't exactly on the road to divorce, we certainly were getting close to the on-ramp.

I straightened up. I stopped drinking and partying and carrying on. I began to put Tabatha first. As I did, I started to see why and how my faith had never developed after I had invited Jesus into my heart as a kid. I had been serious about what I was doing, but I didn't understand back then that while salvation is an event, a moment in time when you are saved, it is also much more than that. Yes, when we ask Jesus to forgive us our sins, we are born again, but that's supposed to be the start of things, not the end.

In Romans 12:2, the Apostle Paul wrote that we should "not conform to the pattern of this world, but be transformed" by the renewing of our minds. That requires unlearning a lot of things we may have been taught by all kinds of "teachers"—our parents, friends, institutions, culture, and the media. As they say in the recovery world, you may have stopped drinking, using drugs, or some other kind of addiction, but you probably still have a lot of "stinking thinking" that got you into trouble in the first place. All that needs to be replaced bit by bit as you allow God to change you. It's a slow process, like the way a caterpillar turns into a beautiful butterfly. It is a wonderful transformation, but it doesn't happen without a lot of struggle and a form of death.

All of that was true for me in many different ways—from how I viewed relationships and success to money and, over time, race. Paul didn't pretend this process was easy. Earlier in Romans, he wrote, "I do not understand what I do. For what I want to do I do not do, but what I hate I do" (7:15).

Tabatha and I went for it wholeheartedly. We didn't want to be halfway believers anymore. We studied the Bible, and we applied what it taught to our lives. Almost immediately, our marriage improved. The next break-through came in our money.

In our first year married, our combined income was around $10,000. Within four to five years, it was close to seven figures per year. The turn-around wasn't because I was especially clever, although I certainly worked as hard as I could. I had hustled since I was a kid: my first money-making venture was a sort of prototype Uber Eats. I bought some cheap hot dogs, cooked them at home, and then delivered them to people with coleslaw and relish for a dollar a go (Mom drove me there). My first real job was at Wendy's. With the money I earned there and from a side gig cutting grass, I saved $700 to buy my first car—a 1987 Chevy Cavalier.

Nor was my great success in my early twenties because I moved into the real estate world, where you can make good money. No, the sole reason we prospered so much was that we started doing things financially God's way. Soon after we started attending church regularly, I gave the balance of $1,000 I had promised. We learned about the importance of tithing and how giving God a tenth of your income is a demonstration of your faith in Him to provide. This is especially true because, starting off, we did not have much; but our obedience was what God honored. I decided to start by giving 20 percent of my income to God.

God supernaturally blessed my work. Before the housing crash of 2007–2008, the property market in the D.C. area was pretty tight. There wasn't always a lot of time to decide whether to buy something that came on the market. God would prompt me to buy this place or that one sight unseen, and I'd turn it for a great profit. Pretty soon, I had my own brokerage with forty real estate agents under me.

The dumpy, one-bedroom apartment was soon behind us, along with the four- and six-legged tenants and the broken-down furniture we had pulled out of the trash and repainted. Now we had a home in stylish Prince Georges County, one of the wealthiest predominantly African American communities in the country. Our home had a fitness center, movie theater, and enough space to take in people in need. Over a period of a few years, we had more than a dozen people live with us for a time.

It was an amazing time of growth. We were seeing the truths of the Bible manifest, not only in our own lives but in the lives of those with whom we got to share what we were learning as well. Exciting as it all was, I knew that there was more. I got to serve the pastor of our church as an aide and armor bearer, accompanying him in ministry and seeing the way he served God. Over time, I felt God tugging at me—He had a change for me. Up until then, I'd been helping people find their own homes; now, it was time to be part of building the house of God, His church—and in a particular way.

HEAVEN IN THE HERE AND NOW

The Bible uses different pictures to describe what the church should be like—it's a family, it's a body, it's a bride, it's a temple. Each of these gives us another way of looking at what the church is supposed to be. Yet another way of putting it is this: the church should be a taste of heaven on earth.

I'm not saying that it's going to be a 100-percent accurate representation. After all, this side of eternity, God is building with imperfect pieces! But people should be able to look at the church and get a glimpse of heaven. That's what Jesus modeled when His disciples asked Him to teach them to pray, and He answered with what has become known as The Lord's Prayer:

"This, then, is how you should pray: 'Our Father in heaven, hallowed be your name, your kingdom come, your will be done, on earth as it is in heaven'" (Matthew 6:9-10).

So what does that look like? There's a lot in Revelation about heaven's physical properties—streets of gold, a flowing river on either side of which stands the tree of life, its leaves meant for the healing of the nations (see Revelation 22:2), and all that. But that is not what I want to major on. I am talking more about the nature of heaven than its measurements.

We know that it is where the greatest praise gathering ever takes place. In his vision in Revelation 7:9-10, the Apostle John writes of "a great multitude that no one could count standing before the throne and before the Lamb. They were wearing white robes and were holding palm branches in their hands. And they cried out in a loud voice: 'Salvation belongs to our God, who sits on the throne, and to the Lamb.'"

However, we don't have to wait until we get to heaven to experience some of that. I am looking forward to rejoicing in heaven, but I want to rejoice while I am here on earth too.

We know that there is incredible joy in heaven, but we don't have to wait until we get there to experience it. We can know some of that joy here on earth now. We know that there will be no more pain and sorrow in heaven, only His peace and presence. We don't have to wait for heaven for that; we can experience some of it here on earth now. We also know that there is complete healing in heaven, but we don't have to wait until then. Through God's supernatural power, we can experience His healing here on earth now.

As the church demonstrates each of these things, it reflects some of who God is to the world. However, there is one more very important aspect of heaven that too often gets overlooked. The great crowd that John wrote about which surrounds Jesus on His throne will be "from every nation, tribe, people and language" (Revelation 7:9). In other words, there is no division in heaven. No racism. One of the major ingredients that surrounds the throne of God is unity.

So here is the question that began to stir in me as I grew in my understanding of God: if it was important for the church to demonstrate all those other wonderful dimensions of heaven to the world, why not the part about people from different backgrounds and places—people of different ethnicities—coming together?

Dr. Martin Luther King Jr. famously said that eleven o'clock on Sunday morning remained the most segregated hour in America—when Christians of different races by and large go to worship with people who look like them. As a nation, we have made a modicum of progress in this area as a result of integration and, frankly, just by becoming more adventurous and confident in moving to other parts of the country to put down roots and prosper. Yet and still, we have work to do.

Many people are not aware of all that Dr. King said in that "Meet the Press" interview,[4] however. Here's what he said when he was asked if he believed that schools and churches and stores should be ordered to integrate:

> *I think it is one of the tragedies of our nation, one of the shameful tragedies, that eleven o'clock on Sunday morning is one of the most segregated hours, if not the most segregated hours, in Christian America. I definitely think the Christian church should be integrated, and any church that stands against integration and that has a segregated body is standing against the spirit and the teachings of Jesus Christ, it fails to be a true witness. But this is something that the church will have to do itself. I don't think church integration will come through legal processes. I might say that my church is not a segregating church. It's segregated but not segregating. It would welcome white members.*

4   Interview on "Meet the Press," *Stanford University: The Martin Luther King, Jr. Research and Education Institute,* 24 May 2021, https://kinginstitute.stanford.edu/king-papers/documents/interview-meet-press.

My, my, my as a pastor and as a church, I don't ever want to fail to be a true witness. It's something that really convicts me and something that I keep in the forefront of my mind.

Actually, racial reconciliation is one of the signs of being a true witness, according to Dennis Rouse. He is the founding pastor of Victory Church in Atlanta, Georgia, where there are around 140 nationalities represented among the sixteen thousand members. When he started the church thirty years ago, his vision was to build it on the basis of the last recorded spoken words of Jesus. Before He ascended to heaven, Jesus told the apostles:

> *"But you will receive power when the Holy Spirit comes on you; and you will be my witnesses in Jerusalem, and in all Judea and Samaria, and to the ends of the earth" (Acts 1:8).*

Noting that the Jews and the Samaritans used to be archenemies, Pastor Rouse saw Jesus' parting words to mean that "part of the Great Commission was cross-cultural. Where did we get the idea that we're supposed to only worship with people of our kind, our race, our culture?"[5]

Let me be clear. I'm not making an eleventh commandment out of all of this. Although I have a passion for my church to resemble heaven in its ethnic makeup, I don't believe this is a requirement for every church. I am not suggesting they all need to be like ours or that they all need to change. Apart from anything, not every church is in a community diverse enough to make such a mix possible. Besides, God is wise enough and gracious enough to use all different kinds of churches—different styles and demographics and emphases—to reach different kinds of people.

Having said that, I do believe that what we are pursuing at Alive Church is very much on God's heart. If the good news of the gospel is, at its core, about reconciliation between us and our Creator, then in the everyday

---

5   Dennis Rouse, "It's a Simple Life: Week 3" Freedom House Church, https://www.youtube.com/watch?v=flTsr436OkE. December 22, 2011.

world there may be no more powerful picture of what that can look like than when people divided by racism are reconciled.

Miles McPherson thinks along the same lines. A former NFL pro, he is now senior pastor of Rock Church in San Diego, California, a thriving multiracial congregation. In his book, *The Third Option*,[6] which tells the story of how he has worked to overcome racial divisions, he writes, "If heaven is diverse, our churches should be too. Churches that look like the kingdom are best equipped to represent the kingdom to the world."

A similar sort of vision grew in me as I began to sense God calling me into full-time ministry. However, I'd learn that seeing it realized would not be easy.

---

6   Miles McPherson, *The Third Option: Hope for a Racially Divided Nation*, Howard Books, 2018.

CHAPTER THREE

DIVIDED BY DIRT

I've been able to travel across the United States and to different parts of the world, and I have discovered that there are lots of different colors of dirt. There's the black dirt I grew up playing in back in West Virginia. Parts of North Carolina are known for their red dirt. Some of my favorite dirt is in Exuma, a chain of small islands in the Bahamas. The sugary white sand there is simply gorgeous. I always recommend its beautiful beaches to those who are travelers.

The texture and color of dirt depends on a variety of factors, from the rocks to the vegetation and the climate in any given region. At the end of the day, it's all just dirt, similar to you and me since God created humans from it. I know we often think of dirt as a bad thing—like when it gets all over our nice clean clothes or when we bring it in on the bottoms of our shoes—but that's not completely true. Dirt is used for many great things. We certainly wouldn't have all the produce available to us in the grocery stores if it weren't for good, fertile dirt. Clay, a form of dirt, has been used for millenia to create beautiful vessels and pots.

When God made us in His image, He used dirt. Genesis 2:7 says, "Then the Lord God formed a man from the dust of the ground and breathed into his nostrils the breath of life, and the man became a living being." The word "dust" in Hebrew is *apar*, meaning dry earth, dust, powder, ashes, earth, ground, mortar.

The world came into being at God's command. As a body of believers, we know that we didn't evolve from fish. We are not the result of a couple of amoeba happening to bump into each other in some sort of primordial soup and a few million years of trial-and-error development. No, the Bible teaches plainly that mankind was created deliberately, uniquely, and distinctly from everything else.

However, you and I are not that different from each other. We may be made up of different kinds of particles of dirt—mine may be darker than yours, yours may be lighter than someone else's—but when it comes down to it, we are all still simply dirt. The color of our dirt is not and was not intended to import status on us—our status stems from our position as worshipers of the Creator, His Son, and the Holy Spirit! Yet we've been letting Satan divide us over dirt for so long.

However, we are more alike than not. We all have bodies, limbs, and organs that function similarly. We all have hair, eyes, fingerprints, tastes, hopes, and dreams. We all have teeth—well, we all start out with them, at least! I've failed at some things, and I am pretty sure you have as well at one stage or another in life. I've made mistakes, and I know for sure you have too, because Romans 3:23 says that "all have sinned and fall short of the glory of God." Our weaknesses and wrongs may differ in their specifics, in their details, but in the big picture, we are the same—fallen humans made in the image of God and needing to be restored to fellowship with Him and with one another.

"We are all of one kind (one biological race), just as the Bible says, no matter the shade of our skin, the length of our bones or the contours of our faces," says Ken Ham, founder of Answers in Genesis.[7] "We always have been and always will be brothers and sisters with a common heritage and ancestry."

Genetically speaking, scientists say, all humans are almost exactly alike. According to the Smithsonian Museum of Natural History, the genetic difference between humans is "minuscule"—an average 0.1 percent.[8]

THE BEAUTY OF HOW ALIKE WE ARE

■ Genetics in Population
■ Difference Amongst Us

The fact that science reveals we are all closely related shouldn't come as a surprise to anyone who knows their way around the Bible. After all, it tells us that we are all descendants of Adam and Eve. When the Apostle Paul was preaching to the crowd in Athens, Greece, he told them, "From one man he made all the nations, that they should inhabit the whole earth; and he marked out their appointed times in history and the boundaries of their lands" (Acts 17:26).

I hate to break it to you—the stark reality is that you are married to your cousin, because we're all distant cousins. This far down the family tree, you might be as black as night while they are as white as snow, but you still share the same distant lineage.

---

7   Ken Ham, *Darwin's Plantation: Evolution's Racist Roots*. Master Books, 2007.

8   "Genetics," *The Smithsonian Institution's Human Origins Program*, 27 Oct. 2020, humanorigins.si.edu/evidence/genetics.

The Genesis account notes only one thing about those made in God's image, and it is nothing to do with whatever shade their skin may have been—it is that they were male and female (now, that's a distinction I approve of between me and Tabatha!).

Voddie Baucham, a former pastor in Spring, Texas, who is now Dean of Theology at African Christian University in Lusaka, Zambia, observes that, from a genetic perspective, we are in fact all the same color. How does he come up with that? Well, it's because our skin tone comes from something we all have, just to differing degrees. This is known as melanin, and it's responsible for our pigmentation.

There are some exceptions. Albinism is a condition in which people are born without melanin. Not only do they have very light skin, but they are also in danger of losing their sight because their eyes are vulnerable to bright light. While albinism affects all ethnic groups, it is most common in sub-Saharan Africa—meaning these people with albinism, who would otherwise be called black because of the group they were born into, are seen as white.

Next, take the Biggs sisters in Birmingham, England, as an example. Marcia and Millie are best friends, as twins often are, but you probably wouldn't call them two peas in a pod if you saw them. While Marcia has pale skin, blue eyes, and blonde hair, Millie has darker skin, brown eyes, and jet black hair. "Sometimes people don't believe us when we say we are twins," said Marcia.[9] "They think we're just telling a lie."

The differences between the two only began to develop about ten months after they were born to Amanda, who is English, and Michael, born in Jamaica. When someone would comment on the girls' different colors as they were growing up, Amanda would answer, "Yes. It's genes."

---

9 Julia McPharlane, "11-Year-Old Biracial Twins Don't See Things in Black and White," *Good Morning America*, 12 Mar. 2018, www.goodmorningamerica.com/family/story/million-biracial-twins-race-define-blend-53681241.

An interesting example of just how alike we are occurred on a British television talk show a few years ago. The guest was Craig Cobb, who had made headlines for wanting to establish a "whites only" community in Leith, North Dakota. He agreed to take part in a DNA test and was given the results live on air—it turns out he was 14 percent black.[10]

"Sweetheart, you have a little black in you," said the host, Trisha Goddard, to roars of laughter from the audience. Cobb tried to blow the revelation off, saying that he doubted the validity of the test. Naturally, he found himself the subject of some ridicule. Bobby Harper, a black resident of Leith, told a newspaper, "I knew there was one other black person in town. Is he going to want to kick his own self out of town and discriminate against himself?"

While I feel bad for Mr. Cobb's error, it isn't an uncommon one for we humans both in the past and present. This is another example of how we allow Satan to divide us merely over our outward appearance—dirt, my brothers and sisters. Simply dirt.

The reality is that none of us have DNA that isn't multicultural or diverse in some way, somewhere back in our family line. "No population is, or ever could be, pure," says David Reich, a professor of genetics at Harvard Medical School.[11] "Ancient DNA reveals that the mixing of groups extremely different from each other is a common feature of human nature. We do not live in unusual times; profound events have occurred in our past. We should learn and feel more connected from that."

Voddie Baucham keeps a sense of humor when he addresses the science of our different dirt. "It's not that some of us are, you know, this color,

---

10 Matt Pearce, "White Supremacist Takes DNA Test, Finds out He's Part Black." *Los Angeles Times*, 12 Nov. 2013, www.latimes.com/nation/nationnow/la-na-nn-white-supremacist-dna-20131112-story.html.

11 Brett Milano, "Harvard Geneticist: No Population's DNA Is 'Pure'." *Harvard Gazette*, 6 Mar. 2019, news.harvard.edu/gazette/story/2019/02/harvard-geneticist-no-populations-dna-is-pure/.

some of us are that color," he says.[12] "No, we're just different shades of the same color. Some of us just have more melanin than others. And I want you to listen to me on this: Just because you don't have as much melanin as I do, don't you dare think God doesn't love you as much as He loves me because He gave me more." And vice versa: don't think you're better because you have less.

Along the same lines, Miles McPherson says that God came up with melanin so that His creative genius could be seen in various shades. "Even what we call White and Black are simply very light and very dark shades of brown," he writes.[13] "For this reason, I believe that we are all just different shades of the same color."

We have let the teeniest of differences between us become this huge chasm. We are a body of believers who regularly asks for His kingdom to come on earth as it is in heaven in our daily prayers. Let us not continue to be divided by something as basic as dirt.

RACE TALK

Given that science suggests there is very little difference between us all, it's perhaps not surprising that the Bible doesn't have much to say about race in any of its sixty-six books. In fact, in the King James Version, the word appears only four times. Each of them has to do with running, not with people's identity—as in how we are exhorted to "run with perseverance the race marked out for us" in Hebrews 12:1.

The word "race" appears more in modern translations—sixteen times in the New International Version, for example. Half of them have to do with running. Of the other references, seven of them relate to "the human race." In other words, all of us without distinction. The one remaining mention

12 Voddie Baucham, "The Concept of Race Is Not Biblical: We Are One Race," *YouTube*, 27 Oct. 2019, www.youtube.com/watch?v=rUyA8TeR1Yg.

13 Miles McPherson, *The Third Option*

of race is in Ezra 9:2, when the prophet rebukes the people of God for not having separated themselves from the neighboring peoples:

> *"They have taken some of their daughters as wives for themselves and their sons, and have mingled the holy race with the peoples around them."*

However, the distinction that is being made here has nothing to do with color. It is based on whether or not they are part of the race that is defined as those who are following God or not. It's nothing to do with the color of their skin; it's all about the condition of their hearts.

That was the issue when Moses' brother and sister, Aaron and Miriam, started to talk badly about him behind his back after he had led the Jews out of slavery in Egypt. They "began to talk against Moses because of his Cushite wife" (Numbers 12:1). Scholars have different opinions on what their beef about this was. One suggestion is that they were upset with him because he had not married within the Jewish people.

Another view is that it was all to do with race—the Cushites were from north Africa and dark-skinned. If Aaron and Miriam were bad-mouthing Moses because of that, then God's response is really interesting. Remember, He struck Miriam with leprosy—her skin became "white as snow" (Numbers 12:10).

Commenting on this passage, Bible teacher and pastor John Piper says, "Consider this possibility. In God's anger at Miriam, Moses' sister, God says in effect, 'You like being light-skinned Miriam? I'll make you light-skinned.'"[14] He goes on, "If you ever thought black was a biblical symbol for uncleanness, be careful; a worse white uncleanness could come upon you."

---

14 John Piper, "Did Moses Marry a Black Woman?" *9Marks*, 25 Feb. 2010, www.9marks.org/article/did-moses-marry-black-woman.

The Bible just doesn't distinguish people from each other by the color of the skin. God sees only one race—the human race. That's not to say that Scripture ignores the fact that there are differences between us. Of course there are. But those differences, our diversity, are a reflection of all that God is in His fullness and His sovereignty. No single people group could adequately reflect all that God is. That's why, as believers, we are called to unity; we need each other in a deep way.

As I mentioned earlier, Revelation 7:9 gives us a glimpse of what heaven is like—"A great multitude from every nation, tribe, people, and language, standing before the throne and before the Lamb." It doesn't say that everyone is the same, like a great crowd of cookie cutters. It's clear that all those who are there have differences that make them "the body of believers"; no one is inferior or superior to the others. I believe this represents the wholeness that our hope is built on.

Notice, though, that it doesn't say anything about races. It distinguishes people by different measures. There's "nation." Merriam-Webster's Dictionary defines that word as "a territorial division containing a body of people of one or more nationalities and usually characterized by relatively large size and independent status."[15] Nothing about race in there.

Then there's "tribe." This is "a group of persons having a common character, occupation, or interest."[16] Again, no mention of race. What about "people"? The definition for that is: "A body of persons that are united by a common culture, tradition, or sense of kinship, that typically have common language, institutions, and beliefs, and that often constitute a politically organized group."[17]

Last, there is "language," which is "a systematic means of communicating ideas or feelings by the use of conventionalized signs, sounds, gestures,

---

15 "Nation," *Merriam-Webster*, www.merriam-webster.com/dictionary/nation.

16 "Tribe," *Merriam-Webster*, www.merriam-webster.com/dictionary/tribe.

17 "People," *Merriam-Webster*, www.merriam-webster.com/dictionary/people.

or marks having understood meanings."[18] Naturally, it has nothing to do with race.

Now, it's true that because people from a certain part of the world share certain characteristics, one of them could be the color of their skin—but this is not always the case. For instance, there are those with albinism. And then there are other people who defy neat categories, people like Marcia and Millie and Tyrone.

I met Tyrone when I was on a ministry trip to South Africa. I joked with him about someone as white as he was having a name much more common in the black community in my homeland. I'd sing some of Erykah Badu's hit song "Tyrone" to him. He'd laugh, and tell me that it was cool, because he was married to an African American.

I was intrigued—and then confused when I finally met his wife. She was as white as he was. "Yes," he explained, "but she was born in the United States, and now she is married to me and living in South Africa. So that makes her an African American!" I had to smile: what a great and beautiful example of how our manmade definitions don't carry throughout the world!

While the Bible may not make any distinctions between people based on their color, it doesn't ignore the fact that we humans do. That's one of the things I love so much about Scripture—it's so real. It is also pretty earthy. Take Song of Solomon. If you think that God is reserved when it comes to sex, this Old Testament book about the romantic love between a man and a woman will set you free. It celebrates the goodness and sweetness of physical intimacy in no uncertain terms.

Interestingly, the young Shulamite woman who works out in the vineyards, under the fierce sun, tells others, "Do not stare at me because I am dark" (Song of Solomon 1:6). The Hebrew word used here for dark is šəḥarḥōreṯ, which means "blackish." Seems like she doesn't want to be

---

18 "Language," *Merriam-Webster,* www.merriam-webster.com/dictionary/language.

the subject of curiosity because of her skin color. She does not see it as something negative. "Dark I am, yet lovely," she says (Song of Solomon 1:5). Thankfully, at least some people agree: her friends address her as "most beautiful of women" (Song of Solomon 1:8).

Everyone needs to know that God does not make mistakes when it comes to people. He creates us just as we are meant to be. Psalm 139:13-16 says:

> For you created my inmost being; you knit me together in my mother's womb. I praise you because I am fearfully and wonderfully made; your works are wonderful, I know that full well. My frame was not hidden from you when I was made in the secret place, when I was woven together in the depths of the earth. Your eyes saw my unformed body

Sadly, our culture pumps out a different message. It keeps telling us that to be accepted, we have to look this way, weigh that amount, have this kind of hair, have that tone of skin. Singer Alicia Keys surprised fans a few years back when she started to go makeup-free after realizing she was trying to conform to other people's image. "I didn't even know my own face," she said.[19] "When I took off all the stuff and I looked into the mirror, I didn't know that person." She spoke about how she started to become a chameleon, "constantly changing so all the 'theys' would accept me." She had been "really starting to feel like that—that, as I am, I was not good enough for the world to see."[20]

Many people, men as well as women, feel the same way. This can be especially true for minorities because for so long, the beauty and fashion industries have been dominated by traditional European styles and standards. I'm aware of some women who have grown up thinking that their hair isn't straight enough, their lips aren't thin enough, or their body type is wrong because they don't conform to the stereotypical marketed image of beauty.

---

19 Olivia Singh, "Alicia Keys Says That When She Went Makeup-Free She Didn't Even Recognize Her Own Face," *Insider*, 14 Oct. 2019, www.insider.com/alicia-keys-didnt-recognize-her-face-makeup-free-video-2019-10.

20 Singh, "Alicia Keys Says"

That is so sad. I'm glad to see the rise of the "melanin poppin'" celebration of black beauty as a sort of counterbalance. However, to a degree, personal pride in our appearance can lead us down the wrong road; it has the capacity to dissolve unity instead of building it if we aren't watchful. Inclusiveness should be the target in any of our celebrations—this is often how and where we learn the most about others. Sometimes, as we celebrate who we are, it can be a slight to someone else. So it's important that we understand that we have all been made by God, and we are all beautiful in His eyes and represent Him. Whether your lips are thin or thick, whether your hair is curly or straight, whether you consider yourself bigger or smaller, taller or shorter, you are beautiful—we have all been made in the image and likeness of God.

THE RACE THAT CAN END RACISM

Having said all that about there being only one race, there is one way in which the Bible talks about race that does divide people. It is when God speaks about His "holy race" in the Ezra passage referenced previously—meaning those who love Him and walk in His ways.

The distinction is not based on whether you are black, red, white, yellow, or some combination. It has nothing to do with skin coloring. It's not about into which people group or ethnicity you may have been born; it's all about where you stand with God. And ever since Jesus came to earth to die for our sins and defeat sin once and for all by rising from the dead, it's based on whether or not you have been born again.

So yes, there is one very important way in which those of us who follow Jesus are different from others. However, it's not about our skin color, and it is nothing that we can brag about, or which should make us feel like we can look down on others because they are "lesser" in any way. Ephesians 2:8-9 makes this abundantly clear: "For it is by grace you have been saved, through faith—and this is not from yourselves, it is the gift of God—not by works, so that no one can boast."

Some people say that the Bible recognizes some races to be better than others because when God brought the Jews out of slavery in Egypt, He gave them a strict warning not to intermarry with some of the different peoples they would encounter—people who looked other than they did. That's a misunderstanding of God's intent, though.

Another misrepresentation of the Bible has been used to justify slavery for a long time. Defenders of the slave trade argued that the black lineage could be traced back to Ham, one of Noah's three sons. In fact, some people hold to this misguided view to this day, but it is based on a very flawed understanding of what happened.

It all centers on the day Noah got drunk. Ham found him naked and told his brothers, Shem and Japheth. When Noah learned about this, he said, "Cursed be Canaan! The lowest of slaves will he be to his brothers" (Genesis 9:25).

First, it was Noah, not God, who uttered the curse. Second, it was on Ham's son, Canaan, not on Ham himself, nor his lineage forever. And, according to the Billy Graham Evangelistic Association (BGEA), Canaan was never the founder of any African nation or race; his descendants settled only in the Middle East.[21]

Refuting the idea that the Ham story justifies prejudice, BGEA says, "Racial prejudice is sin in the eyes of God, and the Bible should never be used to defend it. God created the whole human race, and Jesus Christ died to redeem people from every race. Remember: 'For God so loved the world that he gave his one and only Son, that whoever believes in him shall not perish but have eternal life' (John 3:16)."[22]

---

21 "Answers," *Billy Graham Evangelistic Association*, 16 Jan. 2014, billygraham.org/answer/
is-it-true-that-god-cursed-one-of-noahs-sons-who-became-the-founder-of-the-black-race-
my-uncle-is-very-prejudiced-against-people-of-other-races-and-he-uses-this-to-defend-his-
position/.

22 "Answers"

God's restriction on the Jews intermarrying wasn't about race; it was about religion, you might say. He knew that if His people gave their hearts to others, they would be lured away to follow false gods, with all the fallout that would cause. And it happened, just as He warned. Take King David. He is known as "a man after God's heart" and a great leader, but he also made some terrible choices. He ignored God's instruction and took several foreign wives.

He committed adultery with Bathsheba and had her husband killed to try to cover up the affair. He subsequently ended up at war with one of his sons, Absalom. What a terrible mess because he failed to remain true to the one "race" that mattered—the people of God.

In that sense, I guess you could argue that there is race—one made up of all who are part of God's people—in heaven. There's just no racism. In fact, the answer to the racism we see in the world is the one race we see in heaven—God's people from many different backgrounds. What are they doing? Arguing about who is superior to whom? Fighting about the ways they may have been wronged? No, they are united in one mind and heart, focused on sharing a single message:

> *"Salvation belongs to our God, who sits on the*
> *throne, and to the Lamb" (Revelation 7:10).*

This brings to mind one of the Greek words for salvation: *sozo*. It means wholeness. Wholeness is so much like unity, and it certainly is reflected that way in heaven. *Sozo* is used in Luke 19:10 when Jesus says of Himself, "For the Son of Man came to seek and to save the lost." It's about much more than just a ticket to heaven. It has the sense of healing and wholeness and peace, and enjoying the fruit of the Spirit—love, joy, gentleness, and so on. Isn't that a wonderful vision? It has not a single thought of the division over dirt.

CHAPTER FOUR

DIGGING UP THE ROOTS

The more we reflect on how the small, skin-deep differences between us become such dividers, the more we start to wonder whether someone isn't behind it all, trying to drive a wedge between people. Think of it this way: if there is no racism in heaven, as I have pointed out, where does it come from? Maybe the other place? Surely, if ever a message is from hell, it's one that contradicts Scripture, and racism denies the Bible's teaching that we are all created equally and wonderfully in the image of God.

If there is one thing the devil hates, it's men and women, boys and girls, discovering that they are loved by God the Father and becoming all that He intends for them to be. From the beginning, Satan has tried to convince us that God doesn't want the best for us. He asked Eve in the Garden of Eden, "Did God really say?" He wanted her to question God's goodness.

The truth is the exact opposite. The devil does not have our best interests at heart. Jesus made it clear in John 10:10: "The thief comes only to steal and kill and destroy; I have come that they may have life, and have it to the full."

The devil is a loser in the end, but he's not a quitter. He may be crafty, divisive, and conniving, but he is still beneath the believer's feet. If he wants to snatch away what is good for us, what better tactic than to get us looking down on each other because we think other folks are less than we are? And what better way to ensure that the church doesn't look as much like heaven as it should than by keeping us divided by color?

I'm not one of those people who overspiritualizes everything. You have probably heard these individuals described as being so heavenly-minded they are no earthly good. I don't believe that there is a demon hiding behind every bush or that every bad thing that happens in this world is directly because of Satan. We live in a fallen world, and sometimes we make poor choices all on our own without any help.

But I do believe the Bible when it teaches that we have an enemy of our souls, and I have been a pastor long enough to know without a doubt that that enemy sometimes gets his claws into people's hearts and minds and spirits with really crippling results.

Hell isn't just a state of mind. It's real, and there is nothing good there. It's the place created for the devil, who is the ultimate source of all the evil we see in the world—murder, poverty, divorce, abuse, abortion, and yes, racism. The sooner we wake up to this reality, the better chance we have of changing—with God's help—some of those awful situations. The devil's never happier than when people don't believe in him, because he is free to get on with what he's doing without interruption.

While I believe that the devil is clever—in Genesis 3:1, we read that "the serpent was more crafty than any of the wild animals the Lord God had made"—he is no match for God. Sometimes, we can allow the enemy to make us think that he is bigger and more powerful than he actually is, but he's not really all that strong. I hate to be the one to burst your bubble, but the truth is that the devil didn't make you do it, whatever it was. He may have nudged you and tempted you, but you made the choice in the end.

Ideas don't just float in thin air looking for somewhere to land. They are generated somewhere. There's an old saying: "Where there's a fruit, there's a root." It means that when you see something, you need to trace the source.

As founder of Answers in Genesis, Ken Ham has done some revealing research into Charles Darwin, his theory of evolution, and how that has shaped the way people view race. For instance, he points out that the subtitle of Darwin's influential *On the Origin of Species* is "The Preservation of Favored Races in the Struggle for Life."

Says Ham, "After Darwin 'proved' that all humans descended from apes, it was natural to conclude that some races had descended further than others."[23] Darwin's follow-up work, *The Descent of Man*, popularized the idea of different races of people being higher or lower, more primitive or more advanced, than others, Ham writes. "Darwinian evolution was (and still is) inherently a racist philosophy," he concludes.[24]

It's astonishing to me that such a theory, with such awful implications, is being taught to our children as a matter of fact in public schools across the country.

A SIN ISSUE, NOT A SKIN ISSUE

Because racism is ultimately a spiritual problem, we won't be able to solve it all naturally. When I say that, I don't mean in any way to downplay the importance of working to bring it to an end. Nor am I intending to criticize those who have devoted themselves to doing what they can to challenge and confront racism in individuals and institutions (including the church—where it's often more subtle but no less real). More of God's power to all who are working for justice, just as He urges in Micah 6:8:

---

23 Ken Ham et al., *Darwin's Plantation: Evolution's Racist Roots,* Master Books, 2007.

24 Ham et al., *Darwin's Plantation*

"And what does the Lord require of you? To act justly and to love mercy and to walk humbly with your God."

Look at what was achieved by Dr. Martin Luther King Jr. and all those who marched and labored with him in the civil rights movement. They were clearly responsible for some of the advances I am able to enjoy today. I don't have to find a "blacks only" water fountain when I am thirsty downtown. I am grateful to them and to those who carry on their heritage. However, we will never completely end racism by our human efforts alone because, at the end of the day, it's a spiritual issue.

When you are weeding your yard, you have to be sure to pull out the weeds' roots. If you just pluck off the heads, things look good for a while, but those weeds will start to poke up again before too long. Look at some parts of the world that are crippled by poverty. Corruption, violence, inequality, and other related factors are definitely part of the problem, but there is more to it than that. Even with all the resources that are dedicated to these places, the problems seem to continue. I believe that this is because there is more to it than what meets the eye.

As former NFL tight end Benjamin Watson said, "Ultimately the [racial] problem is not a SKIN problem, it is a SIN problem." Watson made headlines for a Facebook post he wrote after Michael Brown, a black teenager, was fatally shot in Ferguson, Missouri, in August 2014 by a white police officer. Watson's mixed feelings about what happened—from anger about injustice to embarrassment over the looting that followed—struck a chord and went viral.

He concluded by saying he was encouraged. "SIN is the reason we rebel against authority. SIN is the reason we abuse our authority. SIN is the reason we are racist, prejudiced, and lie to cover for our own," he wrote.[25] "BUT I'M ENCOURAGED because God has provided a solution for sin

---

25 Benjamin Watson and Ken Petersen, *Under Our Skin: Getting Real about Race. Getting Free from the Fears and Frustrations That Divide Us: Group Conversation Guide* (Tyndale Momentum, 2016).

through his son, Jesus, and with it, a transformed heart The gospel gives mankind hope."

That is why it is so important that the church rises to the challenge: because it's the only institution that can make a difference spiritually. Advocates can lobby for change, governments can pass laws, and charities can offer help, but only the church can be part of changing and transforming people's hearts.

How are we going to do that? Prayer, for sure. In Ephesians 6:12, Paul says that "our struggle is not against flesh and blood, but against the rulers, against the authorities, against the powers of this dark world and against the spiritual forces of evil in the heavenly realms." We need to be asking God to break the hold of the powers of darkness. God says in 2 Chronicles 7:14, "If my people, who are called by my name, will humble themselves and pray and seek my face and turn from their wicked ways, then I will hear from heaven, and I will forgive their sin and will heal their land."

But we won't end racism just in prayer meetings. Having urged the church to keep in mind the spiritual dimension of what is going on, in his letter to the Ephesians, Paul then goes on to talk about the individual responsibility people have—being truthful and righteous, standing firm. In chapter 6, he uses the illustration of a Roman soldier and his armor and weapons. It is important to remember that Roman soldiers did not fight as individuals but as a unit. They would lock their shields together to protect each other. They were stronger as a team than they were alone.

The same is true in the church. We are more effective when we are a body than when we are solo. That is why the enemy works so hard to keep us apart. 1 Peter 5:8 says that the enemy "prowls around like a roaring lion looking for someone to devour." In the wild, lions will look for an animal that is on the edge of a pack or has been separated from the others. That animal is much easier to attack.

The enemy does this all the time. One of his favorite weapons is the spirit of division. He fires darts of accusation, resentment, and mistrust, hoping they will lodge into people and poison them against one another. You don't have to look far to see this sort of infection everywhere, from churches and businesses to friendships and families. The devil loves water cooler complaining, coffee-time criticism, barbecue backbiting, anything that sows suspicion.

The enemy loves it when denominations within the church divide over doctrinal issues. He loves it when churches divide over leadership differences or what kind of songs to sing. He loves it when employees grumble about their job or their bosses, or both, and dilute the organization from the inside out. He loves it when a husband and wife divide over something—it could be as major as unfaithfulness or as minor as who does the dishes. In divorce, the enemy often doesn't just get two prey—many times, he also gets his claws into the children caught in the middle.

And the enemy loves to see the church divided over and by race.

Why does he work so hard to keep us apart in so many different ways? He knows that, as Jesus said, "If a house is divided against itself, that house cannot stand" (Mark 3:25).

The enemy knows the Bible and, as such, he is well aware of what God has given us to fight with; so he targets anything that resembles unity. He knows that if one can chase a thousand, then two can put ten thousand to flight (Deuteronomy 32:30)! Remember, he quoted God's own Word to Jesus when he tempted Him in the wilderness (though not in context—which is worth keeping in mind when you're not sure if something is from God).

He knows that there is power in agreement. Jesus said, "Again, truly I tell you that if two of you on earth agree about anything they ask for, it will be done for them by my Father in heaven" (Matthew 18:19). The enemy knows that where there is unity, God blesses. Psalm 133 declares:

How good and pleasant it is when God's people live together in unity!
It is like precious oil poured on the head, running down on the beard,
running down on Aaron's beard, down on the collar of his robe.

We are stronger and better together, because only together can we begin to reflect something of the fullness of just how great God is. In Ephesians 3:10, Paul says that God's intent was "that now, through the church, the manifold wisdom of God should be made known to the rulers and authorities in the heavenly realms."

Manifold here has nothing to do with car engines. The Greek word used is *polypoikilos*. It means variegated, multifarious. In other words, it takes a church that is as multifaceted as possible to begin to represent our multimarvelous God. No wonder the enemy does all he can to keep us apart. And I believe that racism is one of his chief strategies. I think he sits in whatever dark corner he operates from and laughs at how we fall out over different colors of dirt and less than a percentage point of genetic difference.

This sort of unity isn't intended to be an optional extra in the church. It's not a nice-if-you-could-get-around-to-it-some-day kind of thing. In Ephesians 4:3 Paul urges, "Make *every effort* to keep the unity of the Spirit through the bond of peace" (emphasis added). Every effort! In 1 Corinthians 1:10, he writes, "I appeal to you, brothers and sisters, in the name of our Lord Jesus Christ, that all of you agree with one another in what you say and that there be no divisions among you, but that you be *perfectly united* in mind and thought" (emphasis added). Perfectly united!

THROWING OFF THE BLANKET OF OPPRESSION

While we're talking about the spiritual dimension of our race problem, we also need to address another important way that the enemy gets in here. In addition to trying to poison the church with a spirit of division, he also wants to infect believers with a spirit of oppression.

Though it's spiritual in nature, oppression is a very real thing—at times, you can feel it when you are in a new place for the first time, or when you walk into a room. It is like a blanket that weighs you down and blocks the sunlight. It tells you that things are hard and are never going to change. It tells you that you are inadequate and you are never going to make it.

And it's a lie. We are not prisoners of our pasts—not the things that we have done that we shouldn't have, nor the things that others have done to us that they shouldn't have. The future God has for us is bigger than the past the enemy wants to keep us chained down in.

I'm not pretending it's necessarily easy. You don't always get to just shake off the weight of years—centuries—of injustice. Attitudes and perspectives get passed down from generation to generation, and mindsets can get so deeply rooted in a culture that many people are defeated before they ever get started. For instance, growing up, Tabatha's environment was not one in which people thought, *How can I get a job?* It was more often, *How can I stay on welfare?*

There has been some leveling of the playing field, but it still slopes badly! It's been more than half a century since the end of the Jim Crow laws that tried to walk back the freedoms that came with the end of slavery—legislation that forbade blacks from using the same public transport as whites, going to the same schools, or using the same water fountains. However, ongoing systemic racism means that black people still start at least a few paces behind others in the race of life because of the past. They are affected by wrongs of history that may have ended but continue to have an impact. For example, "redlining"—discriminatory mortgage lending practices that kept blacks from buying homes in better neighborhoods—was outlawed decades ago, but its consequences are still being felt.[26]

---

26 Tracy Jan, "Analysis—Redlining Was Banned 50 Years Ago. It's Still Hurting Minorities Today," *The Washington Post,* 27 Apr. 2019, www.washingtonpost.com/news/wonk/wp/2018/03/28/redlining-was-banned-50-years-ago-its-still-hurting-minorities-today/.

Keeping minorities from climbing the property ladder was part of "setting the stage for the country's persistent racial wealth gap," which sees white families today having nearly ten times the net worth of black families.[27] And in business, high-level hires are often made on a relational basis, who knows whom—in-groups from which minorities were long excluded. Actually, more than a third of all jobs are filled by referrals, and research has found that "regardless of job title, industry, or location, minority women applicants were much less likely to report receiving an employee referral than their Caucasian male counterparts."[28]

I don't want to minimize the ways in which these sorts of practices can keep people down. However, as Christians, we have been liberated. We can claim what God promised the Jews if they would fully follow in His ways. Moses told them, "The Lord will make you the head, not the tail. If you pay attention to the commands of the Lord your God that I give you this day and carefully follow them, you will always be at the top, never at the bottom" (Deuteronomy 28:13). We have to play our part in this. We don't just get to sit back and leave it to God. He expects us to get up, armor up, and show up.

It's important to remember that oppression isn't just a racial thing. It's also economic. Plenty of white people have grown up in oppression, too, because of their circumstances. Those with physical limitations often don't have the same access and opportunities as those of us who aren't physically limited. What about oppression because of a person's gender? Despite all the advances we have made in the United States, many women are still underappreciated and exploited. It's even worse in other parts of the world. In some countries, women are literally treated as second-class citizens. In some Muslim countries, they are only just now being allowed to drive.

---

27 Jan, "Analysis—Redlining Was Banned"

28 Ruqaiijah Yearby, "The Impact of Structural Racism in Employment and Wages on Minority Women's Health," *American Bar Association*, www.americanbar.org/groups/crsj/publications/ human_rights_magazine_home/the-state-of-healthcare-in-the-united-states/minority- womens-health/.

My wife, Tabatha, experienced the effect of oppression more deeply than I did. Growing up poor, without a father or a strong godly influence in her life, she had no hopes for or dreams of a better life. She never saw herself being successful and happily married because she never knew anyone with that kind of life, anyone to aspire to be like. Tabatha didn't drive until she was twenty-two, when I taught her, because she never dreamed of having a car. There was no set of keys for her when she turned sixteen like many other teenagers. She just rode the bus.

Today, she's an amazing mother, a successful businesswoman, and a co-founder of our church. She has taken some of what she learned along the way and poured it into others through a ministry called PIO WMN, which stands for Pioneer Woman. She shares some of what she has learned about breaking free from oppression.

As I told you earlier, by the time we graduated, we were in debt up to our eyeballs. Here we were, this mixed chick from the projects and a black kid from the mountains of West Virginia, trying to make a go of it in Washington, D.C. Then God intervened, and as we began to believe what He said about us more than what the world told us, things started to change.

Jesus broke the chains of oppression around our minds and our spirits. We identified more with Him and His promises than with what others said we could accomplish and do (or not). And we began to see that become a reality.

I will never forget the day I bought my first Mercedes (or the day I paid it off). Who would ever have believed that I'd drive a fine vehicle like that, or that, in my mid-twenties, I would own real estate worth around five million dollars? What made the difference wasn't just that we worked hard, though we did. What made the difference was that we refused to live as victims because we knew that, as children of God, we were now victors. With God's help, we broke free from oppression.

It's not just the descendants of the oppressed who have to tear down the strongholds of oppression, however. So do those who come from the line of those who were the oppressors. They need to renounce the ways and attitudes that can filter down their generational lines just the same. If we don't pull those weeds, they are going to start to poke up through the soil again. According to the Southern Poverty Law Center, 2019 saw an increase in the number of white nationalist groups in the United States for the second straight year.[29]

We also need to recognize and deal with oppression's evil twin: fear. It fuels both sides of the racial divide. Fear of losing power and authority drives people to try to control minorities who are "different." Fear of abuse and mistreatment causes people to be suspicious of those who are in the majority. Fear clouds our thinking. It causes us to make assumptions. It builds a wall between us and people who are different in some way.

As Christians, we don't have to be ruled by fear. 2 Timothy 1:7 (NLT) says, "For God has not given us a spirit of fear and timidity, but of power, love, and self-discipline." I'm not minimizing anyone's legitimate concerns, which may be based on painful experiences, but I want to maximize God's promises.

We need to be wise and discerning—Proverbs 14:15 says that "the prudent give thought to their steps." However, we can't afford to let fear rule our lives. For instance, I will put on a seat belt and drive carefully when I get into my car, but I won't allow the fact that there are around thirty-six thousand traffic deaths a year to keep me from driving.

I know, too, that some of my black friends worry about being pulled over unfairly by the police when they are driving. It happens, but I refuse to let that make me anxious when I am on the road. I obey the traffic laws,

---

29 Suzanne Gamboa, "El Paso Attack Marked Year of Rise in White Nationalism, Watchdog Reports," NBCNews.com, 18 Mar. 2020, www.nbcnews.com/news/latino/el-paso-attack-marked-year-rise-white-nationalism-watchdog-reports-n1163201.

but I don't keep glancing over my shoulder. I choose the favor of God over the fear of man.

We don't overcome fear by gritting our teeth and clenching our fists. That's like trying to fight fire with fire. We overcome fear not through our own strength but by surrendering our lives to God. He then gives us the power we don't have in ourselves.

The Apostle John put it like this:

> *If anyone acknowledges that Jesus is the Son of God, God lives in them and they in God. And so, we know and rely on the love God has for us. God is love. Whoever lives in love lives in God, and God in them. This is how love is made complete among us so that we will have confidence on the day of judgment: In this world, we are like Jesus. There is no fear in love. But perfect love drives out fear, because fear has to do with punishment. The one who fears is not made perfect in love. (1 John 4:15-18)*

CHAPTER FIVE

THE WHO AND THE WHAT

Whenever I go to speak at another church about "Resembling Heaven," there is usually an awkward silence when I explain that I'm going to be talking about race. It seems like people don't know whether to clap, cringe, or cry. There's often a mix of all three.

It used to be said that polite folks didn't discuss religion and politics at dinner parties because it was considered improper. If that's still the case, then a third topic has been added to the no-go list these days: race. For many people, it's just too sensitive, too loaded, too controversial.

I don't believe any subject should be avoided. The longer we let things fester, the worse they get. It's been said that sunlight is the best disinfectant, but I believe there is one that is even better—the light of God's truth. It will chase away the shadows in which ugly attitudes grow like mold.

I'm not pretending that it's easy to talk about awkward subjects, but it is necessary. There is an art to having difficult conversations. It involves listening well and avoiding the temptation to jump in too quickly with your own opinions. We need empathy for others—a willingness to see life from their perspective, to listen without offering quick answers. In that regard, 1 Peter 3:8 tells us to "be sympathetic."

Too often, we want to respond to people's hurt by saying, "Yes, but. . . ." Then, we go on to give all the reasons why they shouldn't feel that way, or why, in our opinion, they are wrong. That's not empathy. Any time you add a "but" to a statement, you pretty much discount what you just said before. Empathy doesn't insist on being heard; it focuses on listening. More about all that later.

First, though, for Christians who want to engage on the issue of race with other believers, it requires a new understanding of our identity. For too long, we have let the world define who we are. But the way it measures things—meaning, value, worth, success—is all messed up.

Now, I love being black. I can't imagine being anything else, and I have never desired lighter skin. I can't imagine life without being black any more than I can imagine life without breathing. It's just part of me. Being black has certainly influenced the way I see and how I understand the world.

For the longest time, Tabatha felt that being mixed meant she was neither one thing nor the other—she just sort of fell between the cracks. With her caramel skin and curly hair, I wondered whether she might be Latino when we first met. I discovered this half-white, half-black woman who seemed to embody the beauty of both worlds. When asked to fill in her ethnicity on a form, she would often leave it blank because neither black nor white fit, and "other" sounded dismissive. But she has come to celebrate and delight in who she is—she loves being white as much as she loves being black. To me, she has the best of both worlds!

However, black is not *who* I am, it is *what* I am. Mixed is not who Tabatha is; it is what she is. Same for you. Whatever your shade—black, brown, white, yellow, or somewhere in between—it is not who you are, it is what you are. Who we are speaks about our value and our self-worth, our core identity. Having accepted Jesus as our Savior, who we are is found in the cross. Everything else is secondary. The new life of the gospel requires the death of the old self.

I am now a blood-bought, blood-washed child of the almighty God: "Yet to all who did receive him, to those who believed in his name, he gave the right to become children of God—children born not of natural descent, nor of human decision or a husband's will, but born of God" (John 1:12).

Think about that for a moment: my spiritual lineage is now more important than my physical lineage. Mom and Dad passed on a combination of their color to me, but what color have I inherited from God the Father? None, because He is Spirit, not a physical being. Black is the earthsuit He gave me.

I am now also an heir of God and joint-heir with Christ Jesus (Romans 8:17). And I am an ambassador for Christ (2 Corinthians 5:20)—a role that Paul says is part of the ministry of reconciliation we have been given as believers. While we clearly need to see reconciliation between the sexes and between nations and many other groups, there's no more needy area for reconciliation than between people of different colors.

I could go on quoting other verses from Scripture that talk about the fundamentally new identity we have been given when we become Christians (how about Galatians 3:28: "There is neither Jew nor Gentile, neither slave nor free, nor is there male and female, for you are all one in Christ Jesus"?). But I think you probably get my point.

All this means that I am not a black Christian. I am a Christian who is black. The who (child of God) comes first, and the what (black) comes second. The who is the engine that drives my train. Many people seem to have it the other way around. They are more black than they are Christian, or they are more white than they are Christian, or they are more Asian than they are Christian, or they are more African than they are Christian.

I am not disowning or dishonoring or disavowing my heritage, and I am in no way saying that you should not be proud of your background and your culture. I understand too that, for some people, being a "black Christian" is important because church has been such an integral part of the black community experience. For too many years, it was the one place where they could celebrate their true value and worth in God's eyes.

Your color and your culture are part of the diversity this world needs to be able to see God in all His glory. But I do not believe that He wants us to find our value in what we are. First and foremost, we need to be anchored and rooted and settled in who we are. We are His, along with all the others who are different from us. He is our common denominator. Our message to the world needs to be centered on His kingdom, not on our color. I have decided to lead my church not as a black man but as a man of God who happens to be black.

THE COLOR THAT MATTERS MOST

Really digging down deep and laying a strong foundation of our identity being in Jesus won't just have an impact racially; it will have an impact personally. The world is in the middle of a major identity crisis that has been brewing for some time. Maybe you remember the story of Rachel Dolezal. Back in 2015, she had to step down as a local president of the National Association for the Advancement of Colored People when it was revealed that she was not black, as she had claimed, but white. "Calling myself black feels more accurate than saying I'm white," she said in defending the way she had represented herself.[30] She told a magazine, "You can't just say in one sentence what is blackness or what is black culture or what makes you who you are."[31]

---

30 Decca Aitenhead, "Rachel Dolezal: 'I'm Not Going to Stoop and Apologize and Grovel'," *The Guardian*, 25 Feb. 2017, www.theguardian.com/us-news/2017/feb/25/rachel-dolezal-not-going-stoop-apologise-grovel.

31 Allison Samuels, "Rachel Dolezal's True Lies," *Vanity Fair*, 19 July 2015, www.vanityfair.com/news/2015/07/rachel-dolezal-new-interview-pictures-exclusive.

Since then, we have seen the rise of the gender identity movement as an issue, which rejects the biblical truth of our creation in the image of God as either male or female. Instead, it maintains that it's how we feel inside—not our genetics or our genitals—that makes us male or female, or somewhere in between.

This viewpoint is held so firmly that anyone questioning the idea finds themselves in the crosshairs of the thought police.

One accomplished researcher who identifies as "left-leaning" departed from academia because his views meant that he couldn't find a faculty position. Colin Wright's offense? "I question and critique many dogmas on the Left related to sex and gender," he said.[32] "I defend the position that biological sex is binary and not a spectrum. I am also sharply critical of gender ideology because I think it harms women, homosexuals, and children. The Left does not view these as mere critiques of ideas, but rather attacks on people and groups."

These examples from his situation show how distorted ideas of identity are impacting society. Such distortions may not be as evident in the church, but we need to be willing to look closely and admit where our identity is off-center there also. Many times, it can be hidden behind seemingly good motives.

Workaholics find their value in their work. Students find their value in their education. Moms find their value in raising their kids well. Pastors find their value in building a growing church. However, the source of our value should be in Jesus. Only the inventor and maker of a chair can tell you how to enjoy its best and fullest use. And only the Creator can give value to those He has created in His image.

---

32 Marlo Safi, "Why an Accomplished Researcher Turned His Back on Academia," *The Daily Caller*, 13 Apr. 2020, dailycaller.com/2020/04/12/colin-wright-researcher-left-academia-gender-binary.

Whatever may have driven you before you became a Christian, whatever gave your life meaning and purpose, is no longer the source of who you are. 2 Corinthians 5:17 says, "Therefore, if anyone is in Christ, the new creation has come: The old has gone, the new is here!"

When you accept Jesus into your life, He literally gives you the chance to start over. That's not saying that our lives before were horrible necessarily, or that we didn't have some good qualities. It's recognizing that we are neither bound by or to who we used to be, nor are we defined any longer by what we once allowed to define us.

In Jesus, we are united by a single color, and it's not the one of His skin. It's not the amount of melanin that was in Him that matters to me. I don't care whether He was black, brown, white, yellow, or polka-dotted—and I figure that, if it had been important to Him that we know, He would have included a photo in the Bible. The color that matters to me is the red of His blood shed on the cross to make a way for us to be reconciled to God. We all bleed the same color red as He did, whatever our skin tone.

LOSING THE LABELS

If you believe that white men can't jump, then you need to meet Josh, one of our campus pastors at Alive Church. He's as white as the page you're reading, but when there was a slam-dunk contest at a church conference we attended recently, he was the champion.

I may be only 5' 9", but I had always prided myself on my ability to jump back in high school, almost dunking with two hands. As a kid, I'd played basketball hours a day, with dreams of playing in the NBA. By the time I got to college age, it was clear that I wasn't tall enough to make the pros. I was recruited by a couple of small division-two and -three schools to play for them, but I decided that if I couldn't play division one, it was time to hang up my sneakers.

I played pickup games again when I got older and could hold my own, but my jumps were nothing compared to Josh. He was so good when he was younger that he was often the sole white guy on his basketball team. He never really thought about that much. He just loved basketball, and he liked the guys he played with.

Josh's parents had never made a big deal out of color and race, so he didn't either. Through his friends, he came to love hip hop; he still raps some to this day. At one stage, as a teenager, he even had his hair done in cornrows and sported a grill. He wasn't trying to make a point. He was just embracing what he had come to love. For him, it was appreciation, not appropriation. And even to this day, he can still dunk with two hands.

So much for that white-guys-can't-jump stereotype. There are so many more, and a lot of them are centered on race. Black people all love fried chicken, Indians (from the subcontinent, not our First Nations people) all run gas stations or convenience stores, Mexicans are hard workers (or not, depending on what you were told growing up), and Asians are great at math. Stereotyping isn't limited to the color of our skin, though. Listen to some women, and you would believe that all men are dogs. Tune in to certain wavelengths, and you would believe that all police officers act unjustly.

Stereotypes are like a social heresy: there's just enough truth in there somewhere to make it seem believable if you're not discerning and aware. Religious heresies take truth and twist it bit by bit until you're suddenly a long way from where you started. So yes, there are generalities that are true about racial and cultural differences, but that's all they are—generalities.

In other words, if we are not diligent, we will find evidence to support what we have already been told and believe and ignore anything that contradicts that. The experts call this confirmation bias. According to psychology professor Catherine A. Sanderson,

We are more likely to remember (and repeat) stereotype-consistent information and to forget or ignore stereotype-inconsistent information, which is one way stereotypes are maintained even in the face of disconfirming evidence. If you learn that your new Canadian friend hates hockey and loves sailing, and that your new Mexican friend hates spicy foods and loves rap music, you are less likely to remember this new stereotype-inconsistent information.[33]

As Christians, we need to lead the way in breaking free from this false reality. Romans 12:2 says, "Do not conform to the pattern of this world, but be transformed by the renewing of your mind." To me, that's speaking of not accepting stereotypes, among other things.

I do not believe that all police officers are bad guys. At the same time, I also know that DWB—Driving While Black—is a thing. A *New York Times* inquiry found that, in Greensboro, North Carolina, police pulled over African American drivers for traffic violations "at a rate far out of proportion with their share of the local driving population."[34] According to one report, research at Stanford University points to "pervasive inequality in how police decide to stop and search white and minority drivers."[35] However, that doesn't mean that every time a white cop pulls over a black motorist there's a racist motive.

One time when we were living in Gainesville, Florida, Tabatha and I had been out on our weekly date night. We were running a bit late in getting back in time for our babysitter when we saw flashing lights up ahead and realized we were heading toward a sobriety checkpoint on 34th Avenue. We hadn't been drinking, but I didn't want to have to wait my turn to get

---

33 Kendra Cherry, "Why Do We Favor Information That Confirms Our Existing Beliefs?" *Verywell Mind*, 19 Feb. 2020, www.verywellmind.com/what-is-a-confirmation-bias-2795024#citation-2.

34 Sharon Lafraniere and Andrew W. Lehren, "The Disproportionate Risks of Driving While Black," *The New York Times*, 24 Oct. 2015, www.nytimes.com/2015/10/25/us/racial-disparity-traffic-stops-driving-black.html.

35 Erik Ortiz, "Inside 100 Million Police Traffic Stops: New Evidence of Racial Bias." *NBCNews.com*, 17 Mar. 2019, www.nbcnews.com/news/us-news/inside-100-million-police-traffic-stops-new-evidence-racial-bias-n980556.

through the line, so I pulled a U-turn across the central double yellow lines, looking to find a different way home.

Almost immediately, I saw another set of flashing lights in my rear-view mirror: busted. I pulled our Mercedes truck onto a side road, and a cop got off his motorcycle and walked up to my driver's side window.

Now, Tabatha is pretty much the sweetest, gentlest person in the world. She wouldn't hurt a fly. One time we were driving when she saw a squirrel dart into the road in front of us, and she reached over to motion near the steering wheel I was holding, to make sure we swerved and missed it. I don't know whose heart was beating faster after the near-miss, the squirrel's or mine. Anyway, she was really concerned and frustrated that night on 34th Avenue. Or maybe it was her Momma Bear coming out, anxious to get back to her cubs. She was expressing her unhappiness with the motorcycle cop from her passenger seat as I handed over my license and registration. Why had he stopped us? We were just trying to get home to our babies. On and on, all in a tone that was, let's just say, not exactly gentle.

The cop didn't react to Tabatha's outburst, but I put my hand to my forehead and groaned, "Oh, my gosh, she's about to get us arrested."

The cop went back to his motorcycle to check my documentation and returned.

"Here you go, sir," he said politely, handing back my license and registration. "I want you to get home to your kids safely. Enjoy the rest of your evening. And please don't do that again."

I breathed a sigh of relief and drove away carefully. Yes, I was a black guy driving a fancy car, but the police officer hadn't known that; my vehicle's tinted windows meant he couldn't see me clearly enough to register my color. He had pulled me over because I had made an illegal traffic move right under his nose.

That encounter reminded me that there are some great police officers out there. In fact, some of them are part of Alive Church—men and women of different colors and nationalities. One of them is Chris Caldwell, who I knew as a skinny black kid I played basketball with at the YMCA back in Beckley. We lost touch when he moved away, and I didn't hear anything of him for years. He became neighbors with one of our Gainesville pastors, who invited him along to church. He turned down those invites for years before finally visiting one day, when we reconnected. Since then, in addition to serving the community well, he has also become a committed member of the church, helping with our security. Chris and his fellow officers risk their lives for our well-being every day, doing the best job they possibly can, often in very difficult circumstances.

Are there some rotten apples out there? Of course. However, I believe for every bad one in the barrel, there are hundreds more good apples. We have to be careful not to let the few sour our taste for the rest. And just as not all cops are bad, many other generalities need to be taken with a pinch of salt. Not all blacks vote the same way. Not all Southerners like grits. Not all British people have bad teeth (my writing collaborator, Andy, who hails from England, said we needed to put that one in!).

Here's the key: Don't throw the baby out with the bathwater. There will always be fallen people because we live in a fallen world. Just because there is a crooked cop here and there doesn't mean they all are. Many more are civic-minded citizens with big hearts who want to help and protect people. So you still call 911 when you need help. Just because some rich people are self-centered and snobby and take advantage of others to get ahead doesn't mean they all are and do. Many more have a killer work ethic that has brought them their wealth, and they are very generous with it. Just because some churches are judgmental and cliquey doesn't mean they all are. Many more are welcoming and accepting and just want to be part of making Jesus famous in their community.

GRACE AND ROOM TO CHANGE

After the first day at his new job, A. J. Clemente tweeted, "That couldn't have gone any worse!" No kidding. Struggling to pronounce some names he was rehearsing for his upcoming debut as an anchor at a North Dakota television station, Clemente muttered a string of profanities—not knowing that his studio mic was already live.[36] Within twenty-four hours, he had been canned.

Since then, Clemente has gone on to find another television gig, but not everyone is so forgiving. What happens in Vegas may stay in Vegas, but what happens online stays online. Thanks to the internet—to many people—Clemente will always be the guy who crashed and burned live at breakfast-time.

While I love many things about technology, this is one that I am not so keen on—that people's worst moments are captured forever. Wouldn't you hate it if everyone judged you by some dumb or immoral thing you did way back when? That's one of the problems with labels: they want to keep us locked into how we were, not who we are now. Some people can ignore all the good that you may have done and your wonderful qualities because they are only focused on your past shortcomings.

If you were a bit of a wild one in college, they still look at you that same way twenty years later, even though you have settled down and are happily married with a loving family. Maybe you had a season when you struggled with drugs or alcohol. You have been sober for years now, but people still look at you suspiciously. And what about if you have been incarcerated but have since turned your life around?

Oftentimes, our reluctance to recognize that people can change is connected to the fact that they have hurt us in some way. I'm aware of this tendency in my own life, if I am honest. There are people who have wounded

36 Michael Walsh, "Fired TV Anchor A.J. Clemente Explains His F-Bomb Blunder on 'Today' Show," *Nydailynews.com*, 10 Jan. 2019, www.nydailynews.com/news/national/fired-tv-anchor-explains-f-bomb-blunder-article-1.1326078.

me in the past, and if I am not careful, I can be tempted to retreat from them, to avoid them, to protect myself from getting hurt again.

In some ways, it's only natural, but as followers of Jesus, we are called to more. When we are born again, a whole new life and a whole new realm of possibilities open up to us. We are no longer prisoners of our past. We are free for God's future.

What does all this have to do with race? We need to recognize that we can't view all people of a certain group one way just because of the past actions of a few. All blacks aren't this. All whites aren't that. Same for brown and yellow and whatever.

I don't believe that everyone who makes generalized statements about people of a different color is intentionally being racist. It's not like they are setting out to sin. Many times, I think they are just being lazy. It's easier to accept the stereotypes than to dig in and do the hard work of trying to learn more about people who are different from you. The result, however, is the same. They may not be setting out to sin, but when they write off a whole group of people because, "They are all" that's what they end up doing. Writing people off denies them the grace God extended to us and hinders the work God is trying to perfect in us.

CHAPTER SIX

EVERY PROMISE HAS A PROCESS

W hen God gives you a vision, He doesn't necessarily lay it all out in fine detail. That's because He wants us to stay close to Him rather than running off ahead on our own, which we have a tendency to do. So when He told me to start a church in Gainesville, I had to turn to Google to find out exactly where it was.

At the time, we were living in Washington, D.C. It was a happening place, full of possibilities—we had done well in business there and were part of a dynamic and growing church. Now, God was calling us to a small Florida town of around 130,000 people. My sense of anticipation grew when I discovered that Gainesville was home to the University of Florida. Learning this was like getting hold of another piece of a jigsaw puzzle I'd been given to put together without the cover picture to work from. You see, some years previously, we'd been out to California to visit a church where a friend was on staff. While we were there, the lead pastor had a word from God for us: God was going to send us to the college campuses, where His power would be released through our lives.

With that memory in mind, I got even more excited about what was ahead for us in Gainesville. I'm not saying that I saw my future in some sort of movie clip from the heavens, but I had a clear vision—a sense in my spirit more than an image in my mind's eye—that captured my heart. I had a feeling that we were going to be a part of something significant. I didn't know exactly what that would mean, but I was sure that part of it was that we would be a multiracial, multiethnic, multicultural church.

This conviction had been growing in me all the years Tabatha and I had been involved our D.C.-area church. Located in a predominantly African American area, most of the members were black, which made sense demographically. There were a few whites and others, and anyone and everyone was welcome, but not everyone felt comfortable. Like one of my old friends, we'll call him Pete, whom I invited along once.

No one did anything wrong, but with his white skin and red hair, man, did he ever stand out. He just didn't feel like he fit. I was sad that he never wanted to come back again, though I was glad that he did find another church home where he got connected with others and grew in his relationship with God. All I knew when we headed to Gainesville was that I wanted to have a church where no one who was visiting felt like Pete—a place everyone felt was for them.

When God gives you a vision, He doesn't show you all you will have to get through to get there. He wants to know how committed you are. Tabatha and I decided that we were all in. I rolled up my three businesses. We walked away from a more affluent lifestyle and a community of good friends to plant a church in a town where we didn't know a single person; but it didn't feel like a sacrifice. It was exciting to know that we were part of something new God was doing.

We started holding Sunday services at a rec center on the east side of town, with a midweek Bible study in a function room at a nearby hotel. They were both rather basic facilities—we had to move out of the rec center because of a flea infestation. That meant relocating Sunday services to the hotel. We would have to clear away the empty beer bottles from the night before so that we could start worship.

It may not have been fancy, but we had God's favor. Within a year, we had grown to around 130 regular attendees. Then we found a 10,000-square-foot building to make our church home, and soon we had some five hundred regular attendees.

Over the next few years, we saw several thousand make decisions for Christ, many of them students from UF and other schools. We weren't just a young people's church by any means, though—our oldest member, Mama Champ, finally passed away at the ripe old age of 97. Not everyone who got saved stayed with our church—many were young people moving on elsewhere after finishing their studies—but in time, we had more than a thousand members and two campus locations.

Finally, we moved into a new home on our own twenty-acre site. The move felt like a bit of a statement about our intent, because we took over the former campus of a church whose pastor had made headlines for hanging an effigy of then-President Barack Obama outside the building.

He claimed that it wasn't meant to be a racist gesture, but he was objecting to the way the president was "killing America" with his policies. Not everyone bought that. The FBI was called in to investigate, and tensions were high in the area for some time. Mayors from all over the area came to our grand opening as a sign of support for the new day we heralded.

By any church growth measure, it all seemed to be going great. There was only one problem. We had decided from the start that we were going to be a church for all people. As a matter of fact, we said so everywhere—on our website, on all our literature, anywhere we could think of.

However, all people didn't come. It started out okay. I invited the guy who took care of my lawn, who happened to be white, to an early service, and he came and stayed as one of the six original members that started the church; but pretty soon, the numbers tipped. For almost ten years, we claimed to be a church for all people, but we really weren't. We were 99 percent black. Other ethnicities might come a time or two, but for the most part they would never stick around.

It really bothered me that whites would go to a white church, Asians would go to an Asian church, Hispanics would go to a Hispanic church, and blacks would come to a black church, but they didn't seem to want to go to a church together. What about us trying to look like a little bit of heaven on earth? Because we didn't see that, there was a deep pain in my gut, a sense that something was wrong.

I couldn't help noticing that there was one color that didn't seem to be divisive for people—green. In fact, it was a uniting factor. Monday through Friday, as long as we made money together, people didn't care what color we were; they would sweat it out with us. Same thing come Saturday: guys of different colors could come together on the football field while guys and girls of different colors would get together in the bleachers to cheer them on. How come we could overlook our differences to make money or make a touchdown, but we couldn't do the same thing to help make Jesus known?

Something was wrong.

THE ART OF BRIDGE-BUILDING

As I thought and prayed about it all, I realized that good intentions are not enough. They don't say that the road to hell is paved with them for no reason. I don't mean that we were heading in that direction, but we certainly weren't making any progress in going the other way, toward resembling heaven, as I had hoped.

In part, the problem was that we hadn't established a clear identity of who we were as a church from the start—at least, not clearly enough for it to have gotten deep into our culture. Sure, we said things about being for all people in our literature and so on, but we didn't look like that. If things were going to change, I saw, then we were going to have to change. I was going to have to change. Connecting with different kinds of people would mean being intentional about building bridges, and that took me back to my childhood.

One of the best things about growing up in Beckley was Bridge Day. It was a festival held about thirty minutes away every summer to commemorate the construction of the New River Gorge Bridge.

In addition to the black dirt I have talked about, West Virginia is known for its beautiful scenery. The Appalachian Mountains are truly gorgeous and provide great snow skiing and some of the best whitewater rafting in the world. The big drawback of mountains, of course, is that they are difficult to drive through. So this part of the country is riddled with tunnels and laced with bridges.

That is where the New River Gorge Bridge came in—the longest arch bridge in the world when it opened in 1977. They would shut it down one day a year for a big party, with games and food (the funnel cake was amazing). They would let people parachute, bungee jump, and rappel off the top of the bridge, almost nine hundred feet above the water. I remember peering over the side and praying that people's chutes would open.

Forty years after it was built, the New River Gorge Bridge remains an impressive piece of engineering. But it didn't just happen. Three thousand feet long and just short of seventy feet wide, it weighs forty-four thousand tons. That's about one-and-a-half times the weight of the Statue of Liberty. According to the official Bridge Day website,[37] if the planning—the design

---

37 "Bridge Day History," *Bridge Day,* officialbridgeday.com/history-of-bridge-day.

calculations and drawings—had been left to one person, it would have taken them fifteen years of forty-hour weeks to complete. Then, there was the construction and cost—three years and $37 million.

All that to say, bridges don't appear by accident. A lot of thought, planning, resources, blood, sweat, tears, and even the loss of life (just one, thankfully) went into building the New River Gorge Bridge.

The same is true when it comes to building racial bridges. They don't come about by chance. They are only the result of purposeful effort.

While we were still predominantly a black church, despite all we said and hoped, one night I invited a group of around twenty members of the church to our home. They realized when they got there that they were all of our white members in the congregation. We shared some food, and then I asked them how they had found their way to our church and why they had decided to make it their home, even though they were by far in the minority. I asked them, "What does our church mean to you?"

One of the guys started to weep. He told us how he had been an alcoholic and his marriage had been on the brink of collapse when they came to the church, as well as how Jesus had changed his life. It was so encouraging to hear. Others told stories of how God had touched them, too.

I asked them what it was like to be the minority at our church. It was so revealing to hear what they said. They talked about how they had been criticized, ostracized, and even persecuted by friends and family for going to a "black church." They told me how they had not felt welcomed by some of the black members of the church who weren't very warm, but that they kept coming because they knew God was at work in the church and in their lives. They told me how they felt called to be part of what was happening there.

Then I shared my vision of the church being a place that resembled something of heaven, as I would speak about in services from time to time. I quoted Galatians 3:28, "There is neither Jew nor Gentile, neither slave nor free, nor is there male and female, for you are all one in Christ Jesus."

I told them that, while the population of Gainesville was 70 percent white, 23 percent black, and 7 percent other, our church was 99 percent black. However, I felt we had been called to be a church that helped lead this generation as a community of God's people, not judging anyone by the color of their skin but by the content of their character, as Dr. Martin Luther King Jr. once said. I said that if they wanted to be part of that, I needed them to join my G3 team, referencing that Galatians verse I had shared.

"I don't believe that you're here by accident," I told them. "I think God has called us to do something unique here, and I need your help. If you're in, I need you guys to turn yourselves into two hundred over the next year."

I explained what that would look like. Initially, it meant getting more visible. Sure, they stood out to people who were already part of the church because they were different, but they needed to be visible to people outside the church so that visitors didn't pigeonhole us as a "one race" church based on their first glance. I needed them to step up—literally. I wanted them helping in the parking lot and greeting and at every point where newcomers might see them and think, *Hmm, maybe there's room for me here too*. I said that I wanted them to come out of the shadows, to be loud and proud.

There were quite a few tears that night. Most of the folks there bought into the vision I shared—I think I gave them permission to see the church as just as much theirs as anyone's. We finished that evening with a new sense of vision and passion. And sure enough, within twelve months, that small group had multiplied more than twelve-fold.

The change surprised some people who had suggested the reason more white people weren't coming to our church was because they weren't comfortable sitting under black leadership. I'd never subscribed to that, believing that they would come if they felt there was room for them, and they would stay if they found God in the room.

Then, one day, I realized that we were starting to see some of our long-time vision come into being. I looked around the church and saw a real mixed bag of people. Folks with very different dress styles and musical tastes were hanging together like it was the most natural thing in the world. And they all felt that they belonged, that it was their church. I had to smile.

MAKING THE VISION PLAIN

I'll get into more of the nitty-gritty details about how we made the transition to a multiracial church, and how we maintain that dynamic, in the next chapter or two; but the first thing that needs to be said is that it takes intentionality. Vision is all very well, but it has to be translated into everyday choices and actions or it just remains wishful thinking. If you don't change course, you will keep heading where you have always been going.

Tabatha and I ran a marathon together a couple or so years back. It was a blast. It wasn't a walk in the park, though—literally or figuratively. We didn't come up with the idea, put the date on our calendar, and then forget about it until the night before. If you want to run a marathon, you have to put all the miles into your legs, storing them up so they come out on race day. It's the same with any big dream—you have to keep chipping away at it.

In Habakkuk 2:2, God tells the prophet, "Write the vision and make it plain on tablets, that he may run who reads it" (NKJV). This isn't marathon training advice, despite what I have just said, but it's wise. Essentially, God tells Habakkuk not to get all fancy and flowery, like people can do sometimes when it comes to spiritual issues. He says to keep it easy to understand, so someone can take hold of it and put it into action.

This is where people's commitment is tested. It's one thing to go to church and feel convicted in a service about how you are called to bless those who persecute you. It's another to get up the next morning and head into work and face that person who always gives you a hard time about your faith. Sadly, my experience from many years as a pastor is that people don't always want to do the hard work that is required.

I believe that prayer is an important part of seeing a vision become a reality, but it's not enough on its own. In some ways, God often wants us to be part of the answer to our own prayers. He wants to see how invested we really are.

Most people would probably tell you they love the idea of having a diverse workplace. It sounds so positive. But how many are willing to pay the price of building it? Because, like the New River Gorge Bridge, it will not just happen. It's the same when it comes to the idea of a multiracial church. You are going to have to be willing to pay the price—and there is one, for sure.

Part of the challenge is bringing spiritual and physical realities together. For instance, while the church in its spiritual form is the body of Christ, on earth it is also a collection of individuals with their strengths and weaknesses, like everywhere else. In that way, it's a social system that has a culture and a style and a form that has to be understood if it is to be challenged and changed.

A carpenter knows that you get the best out of a piece of wood when you work with the grain rather than against it. That's maybe more true for a church than a business that wants to shift its racial makeup. When you go to work, your boss gets to call the shots. If they decide they want to reposition the business a certain way, as long as they are not breaking any laws, then your choice is to embrace it, suck it up and go along, or find somewhere else to work because your employer is writing the checks. In churches, it's different. People are there voluntarily. When they get uncomfortable, for one reason or another, lots of churchgoers vote with their feet.

Aware of all of this, I knew two things as we started to look at how we might make our vision of the church being a glimpse of heaven more real: we needed to do a better job of casting and sharing the vision, and we had to recognize that, while we aspired to be a church for all people, we were fundamentally a black church. Our mostly black members invited along the people they knew, mostly family and friends who were also black. So, taking Habakkuk's example, we had to take our vision and make it plain for all to see.

CHAPTER SEVEN

BRINGING A DREAM TO LIFE

You probably know that cliché definition of insanity—doing the same old same old time after time and hoping for a different result. After several years of trying hard to lead us to a place where we more resembled heaven, I knew that if our church was ever going to become the one I believe God had called us to be, we were going to have to shake things up.

The best form of advertisement for a church is not television, radio, or even social media. It is word of mouth. That's how around 80 percent of people come to a church, according to research: they are simply invited by a friend. It makes me think of the disciple Andrew, after he learned about Jesus. What was the first thing he did, according to John 1:41? He went to his brother, Simon (who would become Peter), and told him, "Hey, come and check this out."

What makes word of mouth tricky is that most people's sphere of influence is their family and close friends, who tend to share the same racial background. We had to break out of this somehow. Specifically, if we were going to become the body of believers I had in mind, we would have to change our face—in other words, what we looked like to others. That is why I recruited my G3 team to help refashion the way our church appeared to the people we were trying to reach.

People might assume this was kind of fleshly or disingenuous. I don't agree; I think that it was an exercise in both strategic and prophetic branding. Strategic because sometimes you have to force change, otherwise it will never happen; we all tend to follow the path of least resistance. Prophetic because we were making a statement about who we believed God had called us to be. It was an expression of faith—something as yet unseen, but which we believed in.

So we instituted the fifty-fifty rule: for every black person in a visible space in the church, I wanted to see a white person alongside. For every Hispanic person, I wanted to see someone of another ethnicity—on all our literature and our website, out in the parking lot and at the front doors—so that any visitors saw from the get-go what we were about. That philosophy carried over onto the platform. I didn't want just the congregation to resemble heaven, but the leadership and ministry teams, as well.

It wasn't just the outward makeup of our church that needed to change, however. We also had to adjust its internal manner—the way we were as a church, from our dress to our music. I led the way by hanging up my more dressy suits and substituted something more casual. Personally, I was kind of sad: I always thought I looked my best in a nice, sharp suit, but I was prepared to let it go. Over time, I have gotten more comfortable; most Sundays now, you'll find me in jeans and sneakers and maybe even a tee. In fact, when I meet people away from a church setting these days, people are often surprised to learn that I am a pastor.

We'd never had a clothing code that was spelled out, but the underlying style was formal/dressy. That was the result of a combination of things. In part, it was the culture of many black churches of old, dressing well as an outward sign of respect to God. In part, it was a reflection of the church stream in which Tabatha and I had gotten saved and grown in our faith, one celebrating the way God wants to bless His children. It was aspirational: I remember seeing the pastor at the church we were invited to, dressed sharp and driving a nice car, and thinking, *One day, I want to be like him.*

However, I came to recognize that this more formal style wasn't appealing to everyone. So I traded my custom threads for something a little more business casual. In time, that trickled down into the congregation, and others began to follow my lead and dress down a bit. It wasn't about outlawing dressing up; it was about creating an environment in which everyone felt comfortable coming as they were—which is why, to this day, you'll find both denim and designer labels, church hats and cowboy hats, on Sunday mornings.

We also had to adjust our service style. Depending on their cultural background, people can connect with God differently than others. We were undeniably a "black church"—choir, gospel music and longer services. Nothing wrong with any of that, but it was limiting our reach. So we changed things up. We cut down the length of the service, we switched from a choir to a more informal worship/music team, and we traded some of our gospel hymns for more contemporary worship that would appeal to all.

This change was harder for folks than the dress one, and I understand why. Music is so powerful; it sets the atmosphere for a room. Just the other day, I was at the airport browsing in a store that was playing some old school Michael Jackson. I found myself dancing without even thinking about it. And, of course, music can touch our spirits in a powerful way.

We had to let go of some of what moved us to make room for others. We put some of our favorite songs on the altar of sacrifice for a bigger picture. We chose to pick songs and develop a worship expression that could provide an opportunity for all nations, people groups, and tribes to come together in one accord without feeling out of place or that this was not for them.

The point of all our tweaks and changes was not to renounce anything black, but simply to make room for other people of diverse backgrounds.

That has required us to be willing to be seen as what Pastor Dennis Rouse of Victory Church in Atlanta has called "an equal opportunity offender." Building a multiracial church "takes a lot of love," he has acknowledged. "Some people want black music; some people want white music. Some people want me to preach and spit and holler. Some people want me to teach and be very calm and everything. You can't please anybody. . . . The only way we're going to make this work is supernatural love."[38]

The fifty-fifty principle continues to this day: we also have a campus in Orlando where the population is not what it is in Gainesville. We are blessed with members who speak Spanish, Portuguese, etc. It's not a literal one-for-one thing; instead, it's more a reminder that we want anyone who doesn't know us to visit or see something about us and think, *Okay, I could fit in here.* You need to keep making constant course corrections, like flying an airplane. When they take off, pilots have a destination in mind, but they have to keep making small adjustments to keep on their flight path as they encounter different conditions. Without doing so, they may otherwise find themselves way off course at the end of their flight.

By way of example, recently I visited a newcomers class at our Gainesville campus and was surprised to find most of the people there were white. While that was encouraging in one way, as a staff, we also needed to have a conversation about how to make sure we drew in other ethnic groups as

---

38 Dennis Rouse, "It's a Simple Life: Week 3" Freedom House Church, https://www.youtube.com/watch?v=flTsr436OkE. December 22, 2011.

well to keep our balance. It was a reminder that you need to keep an eye on the different seasons a church goes through as it grows.

When it comes to building a multiracial company, there are legalities related to what you can and can't do. But a business owner or leader can still cast the vision for the sort of culture they want to see. And they can be creative. I heard of one businessman who directed his HR department to cover up the names of applicants when they were reviewing CVs. He didn't want blacks with distinctive names that signaled their color to run the risk of having their applications overlooked because of race.

"DON'T GET WEIRD!"

Over the past few years, some other churches around the country have started along a similar multiracial journey; but when I first set out, I wasn't aware of anyone else doing the same kind of thing, so there was a lot of trial and error.

Some things worked and some didn't. It took a lot of energy to do two things at the same time—hold to the clear vision that I had while also being open to revising and changing up the way we did things. When I first started sharing the vision with the church, I suggested that we stop calling people black or white. The point I was making was that color was not our main identity—it was the what, not the who. But things started to get a little out there as people tried to avoid being black and white (literally) about things. You'd hear conversations like this:

Member 1: "Hey, do you know Sue?"
Member 2: "I don't think so. Should I?"
Member 1: "Yeah, she was here at church last Sunday."
Member 2: "Okay, what does she look like?"
Member 1: "Well (big pause) she's about 5' 9". She has manicured nails. She was wearing red pants."
Member 2: "No, don't recall her."
Member 1: "And she's very light-skinned." (wink wink)

Talk about walking on eggshells! Looking back, it was pretty funny, really—people were tying themselves in knots like pretzels as they tried to avoid using the words "black" or "white." We had to learn to lighten up a little and accept that, sure, there are differences that may help describe us, but they don't define us. "Don't get weird!" I told people.

Making external changes like the racial makeup of our ministry teams and our style of worship were crucial, but I knew that we needed to go deeper than just the way people experienced church on the campus. We needed to see the vision spill out of the church building into people's lives when they were being the church out in the world the rest of the week. We had to go beyond just the Sunday service—or Sunday surface, you might say. Real diversity means more than just sitting in the same church building for a couple of hours a week. So I began talking about the need to get into each other's refrigerators.

My collaborator tells me that, back in his homeland, there is an old proverb: "An Englishman's home is his castle." Meaning his home is his own private space, a place where he is king of his domain. If that's still true, then in the United States, it's probably fair to say that an American's refrigerator is his vault.

There is just something about a refrigerator that is deeply personal. If someone comes to visit you in your home, you might show them around the place, even let them peek in the bedroom (if it's tidy). You probably won't mind if they study what's on your bookcases or even pick up a family photo from an end table for a closer look. But you aren't going to open the fridge for them to look inside, and I am fairly confident you would be a little angry if they went over and opened it up themselves without asking.

That's kind of strange really, when you think about it, because they are only going to see what brand of OJ you like, how low you are on milk, and how serious you are when it comes to hot sauces. But the refrigerator is just somehow intimate. It's usually off-limits to anyone but family.

So if you feel at ease enough to walk over and pull the door open without having to ask when you are over at my place, we must be pretty close. That sort of closeness doesn't just happen. It has to be cultivated. You have to be willing to have people come over who are different than you are. You have to be interested in them, wanting to learn about their different backgrounds and experiences—maybe even experimenting with some of their food. Getting to know someone else means asking more questions and making fewer statements. Be careful, though: there is a difference between being curious about someone and cross-examining them!

It means not keeping people at arm's length, which it is so easy to do at church on a Sunday morning, in a coffee shop, or even in a formal small group setting. It means opening your home—and in due time, opening your refrigerator. Rather than keep them on the outer courts, you let them into your more personal spaces.

I believe that much of the racial fear and prejudice we are experiencing is because of ignorance. I'm not using the word "ignorance" in a judgmental sense, just literally—lack of knowledge or information. The more we get to know each other, the more we realize we aren't that different after all.

DISCOMFORT AS A TOOL FOR DISCIPLESHIP

The thing about swimming against the tide is that you can never stop your strokes, because guess what happens if you do? You end up getting carried back downstream. The current doesn't stop just because you get tired. That's as true in the world as it is in the water. And it has always been a challenge for the church to remain relevant.

Most of us get comfortable with what we know. It's part of our human nature—we hold on to what is familiar. We remember the songs we sang and what was preached when we first had an encounter with God, and we look for Him to do the same thing again. We can end up making rules that God never intended. He is always doing new things to reach new people. Think about Jesus' ministry—He dealt with people differently all the time, from how He interacted with them to how He healed them. He did not have a set playbook.

As His followers, we have to be willing to adapt to new styles, new songs, new buildings, and new ways of doing things. That is not being disrespectful of the past. We can and should celebrate our history; but at the same time, we need to be ready and willing to move into our futures. This requires a willingness to let go of personal preferences, to be open to seeing that some things don't have to be a certain way—we just prefer them to be. It may mean that we sacrifice something for the bigger picture.

In some ways, pursuing the vision of a multiracial church can become something God uses to do a deeper work in individuals, because they are constantly being forced to address issues that don't come to the surface as much in congregations where most people share a similar sort of background. When you are all very different, there is more room for misunderstanding to occur and previously unrecognized prejudices and attitudes to come to the surface. It's easy to say, "I'm not racist" when you are not in a position where racial differences are a factor. It's like telling everyone that you are not afraid of heights while your feet are firmly on the ground. Would you feel the same standing on a ledge at the top of a hundred-foot building?

This practice of sacrifice is often tied directly to discipleship in a multiracial church. In order for others to be lifted up, we often have to become loving servants, setting aside our own agendas and personal desires. When there is pushback, this response tells me something about their character and how they are growing in Christ. Do they see and support the intentionality of what we are doing, are they getting the big picture, or do they feel they have been slighted or overlooked? Have they arrived at the space and place in their walk with Christ where they can truly walk in the selflessness that we are called to—to serve the body and one another?

Getting all bent out of shape because you're not given the opportunity to exercise whatever gift you may feel God has given you right now is a self-focused and shortsighted reaction. If you are overlooked at any point in your life, know that all promotion comes from the Lord and never from man. His timing is just and I am a firm believer that your gift will make room for you—at some stage. It just may not be according to your timetable. Being willing to set aside your own preferences and desires to be part of a bigger vision is a sign of maturity to me.

It's been interesting to see how, many times, I have had my eye on someone in the church, recognizing their gifts and abilities, and just before I was about to offer them some new ministry opportunity, or even invite them to become part of the staff, they have gotten impatient with what they saw as their overlong "waiting" time and left to go somewhere else. You can learn more about someone from how they handle adversity than how they handle opportunity.

The truth is, most of us like permission—when we are allowed to do something—more than submission. But I see more in the Bible about laying our lives down in the service of others than I do about getting to do all the things we want to do, just when we want to do them.

I think about how, at the Last Supper, Jesus told His disciples that the world would know they were His followers by the way they loved each other. Why? Because they were as unlikely a group of like-minded people as you could find, if ever there was one. They may not have been racially mixed, but they were just about as varied as they could be otherwise.

Several of them were blue-collar guys, fishermen. One of those, Peter, was a Zealot, a radical who wanted to overthrow the Roman rulers. He and his brother Andrew were also followers of John the Baptist before he pointed them to Jesus. James and John, the other two fishermen, were hotheads, wanting to call down fire from heaven on a village that didn't welcome Jesus (Luke 9:54). They also wanted the best positions on Jesus' team. Not only did they ask Him if they could sit on either side of Him in His glory (Mark 10:35-45), their mom made the same request for them (Matthew 20:20-28). That didn't go down too well with the others, naturally. Then there was Matthew, a tax collector who would have been widely despised for working for the Roman authorities. And let's not forget about Judas, who not only betrayed Jesus but took advantage of his task as the group's treasurer to dip into the money bag whenever he wanted (John 12:6).

Surely only a shared love for God, a desire to make Him known above personal ambitions, and God's love shared among them could turn such a mixed group into a family.

Resembling heaven isn't a one-and-done thing. There is not a special Alive class on the topic you get to go through and then check off your list, along with Biblical Stewardship and Learning to Pray. It's more of an ongoing way of life. I share the vision regularly in my sermons, and I talk more about it in our Growth Track sessions for newcomers, but most of it is worked out in just doing life together—hanging out, worshiping, studying the Bible, and serving the community. I believe that's how life-change— real discipleship—occurs: in relationship. And because we are always having new people join us, it's a never-ending process. Typically, it seems to take people about two years of being part of Alive to really "get" what we are about.

It can be hard work. To be honest, there are times when, for a moment, I wonder if it's all worth it. I have come to accept that Alive Church could be much bigger by now if I dropped the whole multiracial focus. Why keep pushing this thing uphill? For someone like me who is wired to make a difference, who likes to "achieve," it can be tempting to take the easier path. However, I know that, at the end of the day, success cannot be measured in numbers alone, and church growth and the spread of the gospel are not necessarily the same thing.

I think of a pastor in India whose church I have ministered in. There are around four hundred members, and he has taken in some fifteen orphans, which is ABSOLUTELY AMAZING given that he is based in a Hindu-majority population where Christians are under heavy persecution for their faith. That may not sound like much by American standards, but don't tell me he isn't successful in God's eyes. I suspect that, when we get to heaven, his reward is going to be greater than those of some well-known ministers.

Therefore, I have determined that I don't just want to draw a crowd. I want to draw a clearer picture of heaven.

CHAPTER EIGHT

SEEING THINGS THEIR WAY

One of the women in our church came to see me about some problems she was having in her marriage. She went on and on about how terrible her husband was—thoughtless, unkind, basically a real jerk. By the time she had finished pouring out her story, I was ready to take the guy out to the woodshed—in a gentle, pastoral sort of way, of course.

When we met, I got to hear his side of things. He couldn't do anything right by her. All she did was nag and complain and gripe, talking badly about him in front of other people. And sex, forget it—she was not giving him any.

That experience reminded me that things are usually not quite as clear-cut as we think. Proverbs 18:17 nails it: "In a lawsuit the first to speak seems right, until someone comes forward and cross-examines." There are always at least two sides to a story.

The older I get, the more aware I am of having blind spots. Maybe it is a mark of maturity. By the time you have lived a few years, you have probably made enough mistakes to recognize that you don't always have 20/20 vision, no matter what you might think.

Even so, it is easy to forget this and fall back into *I see clearly* thinking. I was in a counseling session recently—no big crisis; I go regularly because I know I need an outsider to help me see the forest for the trees sometimes—when my therapist began to talk to me about empathy. He suggested I maybe needed to apologize to someone I'd been talking with him about because of how I had made them feel.

I was a little offended, to be honest. I explained all I had done for this person, how I had given them things and supported and encouraged them. After all that, they had spoken unkindly about me; I was expecting sympathy from my counselor, not the suggestion that I needed to apologize. After all, I wasn't the one at fault; this person owed me an apology.

My counselor wasn't going to let me off the hook so easily. He asked if I had taken any time to think about how hard the other person had it. Had I ever considered that perhaps it wasn't easy for them to receive help because they wanted to make it on their own? Or that they could have felt some pressure to please me because of all I had done for them? Or could they have had things going on at their home I was unaware of that made everything just too much to bear?

All of a sudden, I realized what empathy really is. It's when you stop thinking about yourself and try to put yourself in someone else's shoes. For a moment, I could see why this person had acted the way they did. They no longer seemed quite the "bad guy" I'd labeled them.

On the other hand, no matter how wonderful and anointed someone may be, their version of events is unlikely to be perfect. In a situation of conflict or disagreement, chances are you won't get enough just from them to be able to make an accurate judgment. For instance, when someone gets fired from a job, they have one view of it. Their employer probably has another.

We have to fight for a clearer perspective. It's the willingness and the capacity to see things from a different angle. An illustration comes to mind from *Gang Leader for a Day*[39] by sociologist Sudhir Venkatesh. In the book about his time studying Chicago gangs, he tells of how mothers in some of the city's toughest projects would let their kids urinate in the stairwells. Gross, right? Terrible parenting. But he learned they did that because it kept the drug-dealers away. That kind of changes your perspective, doesn't it?

Most broken relationships come about when one or both parties lose the ability—or the willingness—to see things from the other's point of view. Perspective is crucial when it comes to marriage, religion, politics, sports, and most certainly, race.

This isn't always comfortable, but it is the price that has to be paid if you want to have a multiracial church. Awkward conversations aren't easy, but they are better than silence and assumptions. Recently, I discovered that someone who frequents our church had nursed a quiet grudge against me for years because, apparently, I ignored her one day. It seems that we passed each other in the building one time, and I did not acknowledge her.

At least, that's her view. Actually, it's not that I did not acknowledge her—I simply did not see her in the first place. There were lots of people around, and while she may have seen me, I just did not notice her. So I didn't ignore her, but that is what she chose to believe, and it has led to her being reserved around me ever since.

Misunderstandings are especially a problem when it comes to race. I'm thinking of an article I read recently in which Marley K., a black woman,

---

39 Sudhir Venkatesh, *Gang Leader for a Day: A Rogue Sociologist Takes to the Street*, (Penguin Books, 2008).

shared her grievances about the "nice racism" she had experienced.[40] She wrote about how, when she and her ex-husband had gone to buy a boat, the salesman had asked a bunch of questions that seemed friendly but which she took to be quietly suspicious. "We could afford any boat on the lot we wanted," she wrote, "but he didn't want to bet on Black."

I get her anger. I am familiar with the "nice racism" Marley talks about—what she describes as "the assumptions dressed up as courtesy, the velvet-gloved interrogations." It's out there, no question. However, I also have to wonder whether she was reading more into the exchange than was there. Maybe her past experiences, painful as they must have been, prevented her from seeing clearly? Maybe the sales guy was just being friendly?

Marley did make a good point, though. "The way to stop asking us dumb questions is to befriend and interact with us, talk to us, break bread with us, and respect us as your equals," she concluded. "Sharing the Earth means sharing all spaces. Racism lives where segregation reigns—and together they're the water and soil where stupid questions flourish."[41]

I agree with Miles McPherson when he says that we may never completely understand what someone who looks different to us feels in their heart. "But you can honor that person by validating their pain as real and learning more than you already think you know about their perspective," he says. "You can acknowledge that people of your out-groups hurt just like those of your in-group."[42]

WATCHING OUR WORDS

One of the secrets to having good conversations about race is curiosity. Rather than presuming or pretending you understand something about

---

40 Marley K., "Questions from White People That Feel Racist." *Medium*, LEVEL, 11 Mar. 2020, level.medium.com/stupid-things-people-say-e3b941476fb8.

41 Marley K., "Questions from White People"

42 Miles McPherson, *The Third Option*

someone else's culture if you really don't, ask them about it. If you're not sure whether someone prefers to be called black or African American, Latino or Hispanic, Hawaiian or Pacific Islander, etc., simply inquire. It's okay not to know.

Unfortunately, the whole racial question has become so charged these days that sometimes we are afraid to say anything in case we say the wrong thing. But that only keeps us in the dark, where we can continue to make the wrong assumptions. It's much better to seek to understand and to apologize along the way if you need to for saying or doing something you did not realize was hurtful.

One area in which we do need to be particularly careful is humor. Although humor has always been a great connector for all of God's people, what's funny to you may be offensive to someone else. For instance, I'm friends with an older white guy who is also a preacher. I am very fond of him. He loves God, he loves people, and in my heart of hearts, I don't believe he is in any way a racist or a bigot. Sometimes, though, he can let things slip out that are inappropriate.

One time, we were together at some church event chatting with another white guy. "Come on, Ken," my friend said to me, "let's get a photo. You jump in the middle so we can be an upside-down Oreo."

Now, I've heard black guys say that before, and it made me chuckle. But on this occasion, it was uncomfortable. Like the time we were taking part in a ministry thing with a bunch of other pastors. I was the only minority in the group. My friend was behind me as we got on the bus that was taking us somewhere. Walking down the aisle, he tapped me on the shoulder and said, "Hey, Ken, you don't have to sit in the back anymore."

He laughed, and I'm guessing his Rosa Parks reference was intended to communicate his rejection of those days of segregation; but as a joke, it fell flat. I felt singled out. To be honest, I truly felt like "laying hands" on him—and not in the pastoral way. If you are going to try to be funny, you really have to know your audience well. Most humor has an element of truth in it, and sometimes, that truth is no laughing matter to others.

As I think about why those incidents hurt the way that they did, it's because each comment suggested that my friend saw my blackness before he saw me. Yet I am so much more than the color of my skin: I am a committed Christian, a faithful husband, a devoted father, a dedicated pastor, and a loyal friend. I'm a man of faith, of character, and of integrity. Oh, and I happen to be black.

As a minority, I am very aware of my surroundings. I know only too well when I am the only black guy in a restaurant. I know when I am the only black guy on the plane. I know when I am the only black guy in the group. So when you lead off with my race, it makes you seem a little narrow and small-minded, in my opinion.

To a person who has not had these experiences, it might appear like I am making a big deal about nothing, but that's just an example of different perspectives. How we are viewed matters to each of us deeply. It's no accident that one of the memorable lines of Dr. Martin Luther King Jr.'s famous "I Have a Dream Speech" is that one day his four children would "live in a nation where they will not be judged by the color of their skin but by the content of their character."[43]

We don't just need to be careful when we're talking with people of different ethnicities. We need to be aware of how we talk when we're just among our own cultural group. I've noticed that sometimes, when I am in an all-black setting, I'll hear things like, "You know how white people are. They. . . ." I am sure the same thing happens when other ethnic groups gather minus outsiders, too. That sort of talk only perpetuates the sense of difference and otherness. It keeps alive the whole "us versus them" thinking that is so unhelpful.

---

43 Martin Luther King Jr., "I Have A Dream," *American Rhetoric*, 20 Aug. 2020, www.americanrhetoric.com/speeches/mlkihaveadream.htm.

Remember, the words we use are, to some degree, a litmus test of what's going on inside of us. If our eyes are the window to our soul, then our tongue is the thermometer. In Matthew 12:35, Jesus said, "A good man brings good things out of the good stored up in his heart, and an evil man brings evil things out of the evil stored up in his heart. For the mouth speaks what the heart is full of."

He didn't stop there. He went on, "I tell you that everyone will have to give account on the day of judgment for every empty word they have spoken. For by your words you will be acquitted, and by your words you will be condemned" (vv. 36-37). That's serious business.

It's not just what we say that matters; it's why we say it, too. What is our motive? See, there is a difference between celebrating our differences and highlighting them. Celebrating them is about sharing; it can bring people together. Highlighting is about separating; it can push people apart.

There is a time for looking back and acknowledging ways in which oppression has perpetuated inequality, if not actively supported it, and repenting of that history. The Southern Baptist Convention posted a resolution on racial reconciliation during their 150th anniversary back in 1995, and I am in no way invoking any of their doctrinal thoughts, etc. However, I could not help but see beauty in some of their resolution language.[44] They started out:

> *Whereas, acknowledging that Eve is the mother of all living (Genesis 3:20), and that God shows no partiality, but in every nation whoever fears him and works righteousness is accepted by him (Acts 10:34-35), and that God has made from one blood every nation of men to dwell on the face of the earth (Acts 17:26). Whereas, Racism has divided the body of Christ and Southern Baptists in particular, and separated us from our African American brothers and sisters; and Be it further*

---

44 "Resolution on Racial Reconciliation on the 150th Anniversary of the Southern Baptist Convention," *SBC.net,* 5 June 1995, www.sbc.net/resource-library/resolutions/resolution-on-racial-reconciliation-on-the-150th-anniversary-of-the-southern-baptist-convention/.

*Resolved that we commit ourselves to be doers of the word (James 1:22)
by pursuing racial reconciliation in all our relationships, especially
with our brothers and sisters in Christ (1 John 2:6), to the end that
our light would so shine before others, that they may see (our) good
works and glorify (our) Father in heaven (Matthew 5:16) This should
be our heart as Christians, no matter our skin color.*

PLAYING THE MIDDLE

As a leader, I know that I am responsible for setting the tone for my
church. It's not enough to just preach a message of reconciliation; I have
to practice it personally. It's not just what I say from the platform that
matters but how I live the rest of the week.

The same is true whether you are running a business that you want to
be more multiracial or whether you're a parent looking to raise children
who don't see others through the lens of color prejudice. Leaders create
culture by their actions as much as by their words.

One of the things I have learned is that, while pursuing the vision of a
multiethnic church, this journey requires a willingness to have hard conversations at times. You also need to have the wisdom to know when to
avoid them. Unless it has a redemptive purpose, conflict isn't very helpful.
In fact, often, it's the opposite.

I learned this the hard way when San Francisco 49er Colin Kaepernick first made headlines for taking a knee during the playing of the
pre-game national anthem, as a protest against racial injustice. I had only
a surface-level awareness of all the details, but I said something about the
situation in a Sunday service all the same. As a patriot who has always
appreciated the freedom I have enjoyed to realize many of my dreams,
I commented about him being a well-paid athlete who didn't seem to
appreciate the opportunity that being an American had given him.

Not smart, right? In hindsight, I see that all too clearly. At the time, it was
just intended as a throwaway remark from someone who has traveled

to many other countries and loves his own. I know many veterans and appreciate all they have given in service to others. I wasn't born with a silver spoon in my mouth, but I was able to get ahead through hard work and determination. I didn't mean to make any kind of pro-this or anti-that statement.

However, I had not done my homework well enough. All I knew was what I had skimmed on my cellphone. I had dismissed Colin Kaepernick as a rich athlete showing ingratitude. I didn't know that he had spoken with veterans about his concerns. I didn't know that his taking a knee was not intended to be a slight but a respectful way of protesting what he saw to be terrible injustice. I had not taken the time to consider a different perspective.

I decided to be more careful in the future. While I love and honor our country's flag, I don't want to let it become a blindfold that keeps me from seeing the realities of injustice. Fact is, I don't need to share every thought that flashes through my mind. And if there is something that needs to be said, I need to be wise about how and when I do. Proverbs 15:23 says, "A person finds joy in giving an apt reply—and how good is a timely word!" Timeliness is so important. The right thing at the wrong time is the wrong thing.

Caution is especially important when it comes to social media. I'm not saying technology is all bad and that we should throw away our phones and go back to using quill pens. Digital communication is a great tool in the right hands. We just need to be careful. It is so easy to see something online and fire off a quick comment without: a) really checking out the details to see if what we have read is accurate and b) thinking through the impact of what we say.

Sometimes the social media world seems like a big mixed martial arts contest. Everyone wants to jump into the octagon and start throwing kicks and punches. Trouble is, there are never any real winners. Everyone just staggers away broken and bruised. They may have landed a few blows, but they got hurt in the process too.

I put it this way: all of us are walking around carrying two buckets. One contains water, and the other contains gasoline. When a racial fire breaks out at work or at home, in the nation or in your community, you get to choose which bucket you use. Are you going to extinguish the flames or are you going to fuel them? Cool heads are desperately needed when things start to get heated. It is easy to lose perspective when you begin to get wound up about things. This is when we need the wisdom only God can give, and fortunately, it is freely available.

I like how Solomon describes wisdom in Proverbs 1:20: "Out in the open wisdom calls aloud, she raises her voice in the public square." The public square was a busy place, lots of traffic and trading going on. The background noise must have been loud, but wisdom's voice could still be heard if you listened hard.

That's still true for us today. There are all kinds of noises out there, but as God's children with the Holy Spirit living in us, we can tune all that out and tune in to what God is saying to us and how we should respond. The only flames we want to fan are the flames of revival, not the flames of division.

Jesus is our great example, naturally. Look at how He dealt with people who wanted to create conflict, coming at Him with trick questions. Sometimes He spoke directly and firmly, though still lovingly. Sometimes He answered their questions with a question of His own. Sometimes He didn't say anything. Sometimes He walked away.

His responses were always strategic. I think of that saying about winning the battle but losing the war. We need to keep the end goal, the big picture, in mind. Paul talked about becoming "all things to all people so that by all possible means I might save some" (1 Corinthians 9:22). When he was preaching in Athens, though he was upset to see all the idols everywhere, he didn't get bent out of shape about it and start lecturing the people on why they were wrong. Instead, he used what he saw as a place from which to build a bridge. He told them:

> *"People of Athens! I see that in every way you are very religious. For as I walked around and looked carefully at your objects of worship, I even found an altar with this inscription: to an unknown god. So you are ignorant of the very thing you worship—and this is what I am going to proclaim to you." (Acts 17:22-23)*

With this in mind, sometimes, I will play the middle.

Someone may ask me, "Pastor, what do you think about those NFL players taking a knee during the national anthem? Can you believe people would do such a thing?"

My reply: "Hey, I'm not really sure what to think or say. I am sure people have different reasons for the things they do. But I tell you what, I am praying for the NFL, for the players, for the owners and coaches, that they can find a resolution that will bring peace and unity at this time."

Someone may ask me, "Pastor, what about Black Lives Matter? (Or white lives, or blue lives) What do you think?"

My reply: "I'm not sure, really, what to feel or think about that. But I know that God knows best. I just pray that we all find His will, and that we do what we can to love people in spite of their race, or in spite of what they do or don't do."

Someone may ask me, "Pastor, what do you think about that police shooting? Can you believe that blacks are being gunned down still in our day and age?"

My reply: "I feel absolutely awful about that. I am horrified by any unnec-essary loss of life. I am praying for the family of those who have lost a loved one, and I am also praying for the officers who have been accused, that God will bring about justice, and help us all find His will and way during all of this."

After all, who said that we have to choose sides on everything? Could it be that neither the Republicans nor the Democrats are right about everything? I'm the guy who hates labels, who doesn't want to be stereotyped. I typically lean one way in my worldview and my voting, but I am a registered independent. Why? Because as a leader, I don't want people to label me one way or another.

One time, I had a guy from my church pull me to the side. He was a great partner in the ministry, a faithful servant, and someone I considered a personal friend. He came to me so disturbed and concerned that, from a comment I had made, I must vote differently than the way he did. He was feeling like he would have to leave the church as a result. Really? Because he and the pastor didn't vote the same way? God forbid that someone's loyalty to His house should be only a vote away from ending.

To be fair, I used to think the same way to a degree. I'd be like, "How can you say you are a Christian and vote for so-and-so? There must be something wrong with you." I've come to see that as short-sighted. If you can work somewhere the owner votes a different way than you do, then you should be able to worship at a church where the pastor and you don't see eye to eye on everything. They are your spiritual leader, not your political consultant.

I'm not saying that politics is unimportant. What we believe about life and the world matters and informs the decisions we make. Our understanding of who God is and how His world works best is shaped by our faith. Being a Christian isn't just fire insurance for the hereafter; it's about how to live in the here and now, and that has practical implications for what we think about society, government, and law.

However, the church is, first and foremost, His body, not a political assembly. And we need to be more focused on what brings us together—lifting up His name and sharing the good news of salvation—than the things that can divide us, like race and politics.

CHAPTER NINE

BUMPS AND BRUISES ON THE ROAD TO RACIAL RECONCILIATION

There has been racial reconciliation happening here in the members of Alive. Melanie, a white woman in her fifties who is now one of our pastors, recalls her family being threatened with cross burnings when she was young. Their offense: being a white family with black friends. This was just back in the eighties, mind, well after the civil rights era, but what she calls "unspoken segregation" was still the order of the day. "You were on one side of the tracks, and they were on the other, and you didn't talk to each other, and that was that."

Except Melanie grew up in a Christian family that believed people were all the same no matter their color, and they lived like it. That didn't go down too well in some of the rural Florida towns they lived in. Neither did the mixed singing group they traveled around with. When some churches learned that two of the kids in the group were black, they wouldn't let the non-whites in.

"So Mom and Dad would say, 'Well then, I guess we're not coming in either,'" Melanie recalls. "We'd all go back to our house, and my folks would put on some music and get some chips and soda pop, and we'd have a little party instead."

Melanie found that kind of prejudice to be more widespread than she first thought. When she toured the country with a performing arts group, the organizers switched out her usual dance partner, who was black, for one of the white guys in the group in some Southern states to avoid hassles.

When she started attending our church in Gainesville with her then-boyfriend, Neil, they were the only white couple in the congregation. "People would ask me, 'Why are you going to that black church?'" she says. "And I would tell them, 'Well, it's not a black church if we are there, right?'"

She had always attended churches that had different ethnic groups in them because that was important to her. But she'd never heard much about the importance of church resembling heaven to better reflect what God is like until she heard me talking about it.

"It was so appealing to me," she says. "I wanted to help make it happen: a place where we can all come together and worship and love one another, whether it's a black man married to a white woman, or reverse, or a Mexican married to a white, or whatever—polka-dotted person married to a striped person. You can come to Alive and feel that you won't be judged, that you won't have a label put on you. There are very few places you can go like that."

Melanie knows that it isn't always easy. "You can't be afraid to have the hard conversations. You can't be all (put your fingers in your ears and go), 'La-la-la, we're all the same.' You have to talk about the differences."

CHANGING THE VOCABULARY

Even with a commitment to being part of a diverse church, there can be misunderstandings and hurt feelings. Since coming on staff, there have been times when Melanie has heard that she's only in her position because of her race.

"It upsets me because I can't stand that supremacy kind of thing," she says. "It goes back to when I was a teenager and white people would get on me for having a black friend. It just makes my skin crawl. So when people say something like that about me, I usually go to one of the other pastors and ask them to help me deal with it because I don't want to stay mad."

One time, a black member of the church with whom Melanie was close posted something on social media about race. Melanie posted a comment she intended to be supportive, saying that she had been raised to be color-blind, and that everyone was equal. That was not how her words were taken.

The other woman responded angrily, saying that she was offended by what Melanie had said, and that she was proud to be an African American. "I read it and just started crying," Melanie remembers. "It upset me so much. Like, what had I done? And why didn't she just call me to talk about it? I thought I was saying something nice."

When Melanie came to me about this, I had to encourage her to keep going, despite the hurt she felt—to accept that she wouldn't always get it right, but I knew that her heart was in the right place.

"It was a real reminder of how tender this area is," Melanie says. "And there have been a few other occasions when I have said something as a white that has come across differently than what I meant. You have to keep going after the difficult conversations, though. You just have to be able to say, 'I'm sorry, I didn't mean to offend you, so help me out. How should I say that?'"

Melanie has retired the phrase "color-blind" from her language when it comes to race. "Even though your intent may be good and pure, when you recognize it's not helpful, you just have to take it out of your vocabulary."

For all the bumps along the way, Melanie has enjoyed the journey we have been on. "It's truly been a great thing to be part of all this," she says, "to see people come and feel comfortable and want to come back because they see the diversity. It's a joy to be part of a church that resembles heaven."

Crystal, an attorney, has been part of the Alive story for many years, too. She is an African American who was very aware of race as an issue growing up in Tennessee. "There were things we could not do or special ways we had to behave or conduct ourselves because we were black."

Her parents worked hard to be able to send her and her brother to private school. For most of her elementary education, Crystal was the only black child in her grade. In middle and high school, if you were a black student there, "it was probably because you were athletic or your parents were wealthy. I was neither, so I didn't really fit in." Nor did she fit at the black inner-city church she attended, "because I spoke grammatically-correct English, and didn't attend any of the schools or functions that the other kids did."

All of this made her aware of color, "but it wasn't necessarily an issue. I remember writing a paper in the seventh grade about how I wasn't African American because I had never been to Africa, and I had no plans of going. I was an American who happened to have darker skin."

White friends would laugh at the bonnet she wore overnight at slumber parties. They called it her "Oprah Winfrey hat." But though she felt a bit different, it didn't bother her too much until she got older and was passed over for positions and roles in the school because of her color. "No matter how hard I tried, there were people who did not want me to succeed because I was black, and it became evident the older that I got."

As far as church went, to her there were white ones and black ones, and that was just the way it was. "There was no crossover or mixing. We liked gospel. 'They' liked Michael W. Smith and DC Talk. It was just different, and the worlds did not collide but we were all 'Christians.'"

THE IMPORTANCE OF INTENTIONALITY

Then Crystal came to our church in Gainesville. "One of the coolest things I've seen is witnessing the fruits of our declarations," she told me. "We were a 'black' church for a long time, if you looked at the numbers. But we believed that it was God's intent to have a church on earth that reflected the diversity of heaven. So we declared it, we believed it, and we were intentional about it"—the fifty-fifty principle being an important part of that. "Now, we have an incredibly diverse church, with a black lead pastor in the South! I love it!"

Crystal says that her perspective on the importance of intentional diversity has changed. "In spite of my experiences as a black woman in America, I've always embraced my individuality and that of those around me, regardless of color. But when you understand the heart of the Father, you realize that the segregation on Sunday perpetuates the race problem in our nation.

"God created each of us uniquely in His own image, and if we want the world to embrace this ideal, the church needs to be the forerunner. Why is it that we have fought to have diversity in schools and diversity in our workplaces, but not in the church? We should be able to worship together like any other day and stop using our 'preferences' as an excuse to divide us. God blesses our unity, yet there is so much division in our society. To correct this, we must be intentional about our diversity."

Race wasn't that much of an issue to Anthony, as we'll call him, when he was growing up in New York City. His parents were born and raised in Jamaica, and he lived in a mostly-black neighborhood and attended a largely black school. "As a child, I was mostly blind to race, but as I got older, I experienced and witnessed some things that helped me learn that it is an issue in America."

Moving to Florida and living and going to school in predominantly white communities was eye-opening; Anthony developed a close relationship with the white kid next door, who he now considers "a little brother."

Although he grew up in church, kind of like me, Anthony didn't get serious or personal about his faith until he was in college. "My views on race didn't change a whole lot at first, but over time they did," he says. "As I was taught more on race and how heaven will be diverse, full of people from every nation, it helped frame a better view for me."

One of his big lessons has been learning that people who have "negative or poisonous mindsets" about race were probably taught these things, "and that it's not directed at me personally." He has also had the satisfaction of some "cringing moments," when someone who has gotten to know him has told him he is different from what they had expected—proof that "one person can begin to help tear down prejudices."

"More people need to hear the message of church resembling heaven," Anthony says. That means "educating and demonstrating that the kingdom of God doesn't follow the rules of this world," and teaching about the beauty of diversity. "It's an important topic."

Racial diversity isn't a new idea to Leslie, a Latina Alive member. "My older sister is half-black, and my twin and I are half-white, so we were always taught to love one another no matter what, which I believe translated to us as adults being open and loving to everyone," she says. "Interacting with other ethnic groups was the same as interacting with people of my same ethnic group. It was never a problem."

What has changed since she became a Christian a few years ago is her understanding of how important diversity is to God. "The world is already divided by race and it has caused separation and animosity between different races," Leslie says. "The responsibility of the church is to make sure we are leading the way in making people one. There should be no division in the church, but we have to be intentional in bringing diversity to the church. It doesn't just happen."

REMEMBERING THE GOAL

Scott finds that being the executive pastor at Alive is tougher than any other ministry position he has held. "Being part of an intentionally diverse church can be a struggle," he admits. "We live in a society that doesn't want to talk about race, but unless we do, we are going to keep bringing up those stereotypes that separate us."

Scott was raised in a Christian home, and he grew up in an almost-exclusively-white environment which wasn't necessarily known for building up others that looked different. "I was taught and indoctrinated into a mindset that looked at people who were different colors than I was and considered them lesser," he recalls. "I heard them referred to as thugs or troublemakers, people who couldn't have the same moral values and character that I did."

Things started to change when he went to college, thanks to a football player called Cedric. The two met in the gym, where Scott was working out to be ready for another of the fights he found himself getting into because of the way he was living at the time.

"I've got your back," Cedric told him one day. Scott didn't really want anything to do with Cedric, given that he was black; but over time, a friendship developed between the two and one of Cedric's friends. "They would just come by my door every couple of days to say hi and check in with me," Scott says. "It was like, 'Oh, so you're not all those things that had been put into my heart when I was growing up.' Once I started having exposure and experiences that contradicted what I was brought up with, my heart began to change. It helped me step into a place where I was able to see what had been planted in my mind as a child did not have to be passed on to my kids."

Scott and his wife began to make sure that their four children were introduced to different ethnicities and cultures, but they wanted more than they found in the mostly-white churches they had experienced. That brought them to Alive. "I wanted us to be part of a church that was diverse," he told me. "A lot of churches reach only one demographic. I'm not saying that's wrong, but I think that we are called to do something more. I don't want to segregate the gospel by color. I want a church of all colors and all ages."

Scott knows as well as anyone that reaching for a dream can be hard work. He has been open about his family's prejudiced background. It has not made his job as executive pastor easy. He often encounters situations that can be full of tension. He had to handle things when a black member of Alive told the white lady who oversaw the children's ministry that she couldn't speak into a situation there because she didn't understand how to raise black kids.

"I wanted to be self-righteous," Scott admits of those kinds of situations, "but at the same time, I know that I had some of the same kinds of biases growing up. You have to be able to put aside how you feel and just talk to someone as an individual and try to hear them."

It can be hard, he says. "I am like, 'Okay, I want to listen to what you are saying. But at the same time, I feel like you have to give me a chance. I'm here, and I am not going anywhere.' You just have to be willing to have those tough conversations and see them through to understanding, trusting the Spirit to be present at all times."

Those challenging talks aren't just with church members—they are also between staff and leadership. Though Scott is committed to the vision I carry for Alive, we don't always understand each other or see eye to eye on everything.

"We still come from different cultural backgrounds," he says of our relationship. "But if we can't have these conversations, if we can't look at each other and say, 'Hey, is this a cultural thing or is this just my opinion? Help me understand,' then we can't expect people in the church to have them."

Being willing to keep doing the personal reflection that reaching across the racial divide requires is vital, but it's not enough to sustain you over the long haul. To keep going, you need more than just determination. You need a clear picture of where you are heading, your destination, one that makes all the bumps and blisters worth it. That is what Paul had in mind when he wrote, "Forgetting what is behind and straining toward what is ahead, I press on toward the goal to win the prize for which God has called me heavenward in Christ Jesus" (Philippians 3:13-14).

"It's cool when you bring all these different cultures together and put them aside for something greater," says Scott. "You get these individuals under one roof and say, 'We're not here as Republicans or Democrats, black or white, old or young. We are here for Jesus.'

"Nothing speaks more of the gospel, for me. I want to be part of a church that looks a little like heaven. There's no greater vision than that."

CHAPTER TEN

THE ACID TEST

A sk people these days if they are racist, and most would probably deny it. Most of those who say that would be sincere, but the thing about racism is that it can be kind of subtle. They may not consciously look down on other people because of their color, but prejudice can creep into your beliefs and attitudes without you even realizing it.

For me, the acid test is when it comes to interracial marriage. Again, most people would probably say they don't have a problem with it; you love who you love, and that's okay. Until the issue comes knocking at their own front door: when someone of another color arrives to marry their son or daughter. That's when racial acceptance stops being a vague principle and becomes a very real personal issue. In that regard, I sometimes wonder how far we have come from the days of Richard and Mildred Loving.

A Hollywood scriptwriter couldn't have chosen a better last name for a couple whose only crime was to have fallen for someone with different-colored skin. Yet they were effectively exiled from Virginia in 1959 for breaking the state's Racial Integrity Act, a law banning marriage between blacks and whites.[45] Richard (white) and Mildred (black and Native American) challenged the ruling, which was overturned by an historic Supreme Court decision in 1967 that led to similar laws in sixteen other states also being ruled unconstitutional.

That may sound like ancient history, but just over twenty years ago, there was a big break between two senior Christian leaders when one of them, a black pastor, learned that the other ministry had broadcast teaching that said that young white Christians should not date people of other races.[46]

Stephen Strang, the editor and publisher of *Charisma* magazine, which reported on the fallout, said, "There is only one race—the human race. To me, the question of interracial marriage is a non-issue. The Bible only forbids Christians to marry unbelievers."[47]

The subtle attitude that caused that split still lingers today. I know of one white pastor of a big-name church whose daughter married a black South African. The pastor had friends come to him and ask if he was cool with that—did he have any concerns? His answer: "Does he love my daughter?" While most folks wouldn't come right out and say they believe interracial marriage is wrong, you might be surprised by how often I am asked what I think about the issue. The question is asked thoughtfully and with a tone of humility, along these lines:

"Pastor, I'm not racist or anything like that, you understand. It's just that I wouldn't want my son or daughter to have to deal with all the problems that can come with an interracial marriage, you know? That's the only reason I would prefer them not to marry someone of a different color."

45 "Richard Loving." *Biography.com*, A&E Networks Television, 12 June 2020, www.biography.com/activist/richard-loving.

46 John Dart, "Issue of Racism Breaks Ties That Bound Two Churches," *Los Angeles Times*, 28 Mar. 1998, https://www.latimes.com/archives/la-xpm-1998-mar-28-me-33511-story.html.

47 Dart, "Issue of Racism Breaks"

At one level, it all sounds so reasonable—and even caring. But, you know what? Life is full of problems. If you don't want your children to have any problems, then don't let them grow up and don't let them out of the house. Part of being a Christian is taking up our cross and following Jesus, living as faithful witnesses in a world that does not recognize Him as Lord.

In fact, Jesus Himself told us, "In this world you will have trouble. But take heart! I have overcome the world" (John 16:33). So let's not use "avoiding trouble" as an excuse for harboring quiet prejudice.

I mentioned earlier in the book John Piper's comments on how God turned Miriam "whiter"—giving her leprosy—when she grumbled about Moses marrying a dark-skinned woman. For Pastor Piper, opposing interracial marriage is "one of the deepest roots of racial distance, disrespect, and hostility."[48] He tears into the "life will be hard" argument:

> It's a catch-22. It's like the army being defeated because there aren't enough troops, and the troops won't sign up because the army's being defeated. Oppose interracial marriage, and you will help create a situation of racial disrespect. And then, since there is a situation of disrespect, it will be prudent to oppose interracial marriage.
>
> Here is where Christ makes the difference. Christ does not call us to a prudent life, but to a God-centered, Christ-exalting, justice-advancing, counter-cultural, risk-taking life of love and courage. Will it be harder to be married to another race, and will it be harder for the kids? Maybe. Maybe not. But since when is that the way a Christian thinks? Life is hard. And the more you love the harder it gets.[49]

If that was hard for you to digest in any way, I pray that you make it to Chapter 11, because there is more for you there to help really bring this home.

---

48 John Piper, "Did Moses Marry ?"
49 John Piper, "Did Moses Marry ?"

For the record, my answer to people when they ask me the interracial marriage question is similar to Stephen Strang's. "I don't think there is any problem at all with interracial marriage," I will tell them. But then I like to get a little sassy for a moment. "Unless" I add, and then I pause to let them think maybe there is a get-out clause.

"Unless their name is Chewbacca"—who you may remember was Hans Solo's tall, hairy sidekick in *Star Wars*, a Wookie from the planet Kashyyyk. "Then we have something of a problem," I will go on, "because we're not talking about supposed 'different races,' we're talking about different species, and the Bible is very clear about that. As long as they are a homo sapien, you are good to go."

Actually, for Christians there is one other legitimate concern when it comes to marriage—that their son or daughter finds another believer. Scripture is clear that being "unequally yoked," when one person is a Christian and the other is not, is not a good foundation for a marriage or a family.

I have two daughters and a son, and while we are a long way from their marrying years, I don't care one lick about the color of the skin of the person they choose to spend the rest of their life with. You know what I am concerned about? That their spouse:

- is a born-again believer who wants to live their lives by the principles of God's Word
- is a person of character
- is a person of honor
- is a person of integrity
- loves God more than they love my child
- loves and respects them
- shares a vision and passion to serve Jesus together

The rest is just more or less melanin—as far as I am concerned.

How about you and the acid test? Take a moment to pause and seriously consider the question: How would you feel if your son or daughter announced they were planning to marry someone of a different color? Don't just give the knee-jerk "right answer." Think through all that it would mean, and answer the question honestly. It might be revealing.

SIGNS OF HOPE, SIGNS OF RESISTANCE

It can be lonely when you are exploring new territory. If multiracial churches are uncommon, then those led by black pastors are even more unusual. Therefore, I have been encouraged to find other pastors out there, black and white, who share a similar desire to break down racial barriers and see their churches look more like Revelation 7:9.

A couple of years ago, I was privileged to be part of a summit organized by John Gray, pastor of Relentless Church in Greenville, South Carolina. He took some heat from other black pastors for meeting with President Donald Trump to talk about prison reform and job creation, two issues of great concern to the black community.

Pastor Gray dismissed the idea that sitting down with someone meant you agreed with everything that they said or believed; look at how Jesus interacted with people. "My job is to drive the dialogue not only into the natural but the spiritual and to identify areas where the church can be an agent of healing as opposed to a place of further division," Pastor Gray said.[50]

I got to be part of the event with a group of pastors involved in multiracial ministry including Dr. A. R. Bernard, leader of Christian Cultural Center in Brooklyn, New York; Steven Furtick, lead pastor of Elevation Church in Charlotte, North Carolina; and Pastor Levi Lusko of Fresh Life Church in Kalispell, Montana. From that event, Pastor Gray launched The Bridge,

---

50 Leonardo Blair, "Pastor John Gray unites with megachurch leaders to push bridging racial divide," *The Christian Post,* 16 Nov. 2018, https://www.christianpost.com/news/pastor-john-gray-unites-megachurch-leaders-push-bridging-racial-divide.html..

a movement to encourage the kind of hard conversations about race I also advocate.

There are good things happening elsewhere, like Victory Church in Atlanta, Georgia. Converge Church in Moorestown, New Jersey, was formed in 2018 when Destiny Church, a mostly African American congregation, merged with Maranatha Christian Fellowship, where most members were Caucasian. "We're actually living out what Dr. King talked about," said Jonathan Leath, one of the co-pastors.[51] "We do not want Sunday to continue to be the most segregated day of the week."

Then there is the Mosaix Global Network's Multiethnic Church Conference. It meets every three years to bring together pastors to share their stories and struggles and strategies in leading multiethnic churches. The network was co-founded by Mark DeYmaz, who started a multiethnic church in Little Rock, Arkansas, in 2001, "after he grew bothered that the only people of color at the church where he had long served were janitors."[52] For DeYmaz, some discomfort is simply the price that has to be paid for growing a racially mixed church. "We embrace the tension, and that's very different than the normative church, which is trying to make everybody comfortable," he says.[53]

These sorts of positive examples are part of a welcome trend. The percentage of multiracial congregations in the United States is more than double what it was just over twenty years ago. Around 20 percent of people who attend church or some other religious service go to a place of worship that is mixed racially.[54] A Baylor University study in 2018 found that 12 percent of all congregations nationwide were multiracial, while

51 Kelly Flynn, et al., "MLK Has a Dream Once 'Moore'," *The Sun Newspapers*, 7 Jan. 2020, thesunpapers.com/2020/01/07/mlk-has-a-dream-once-moore/.

52 Adelle M. Banks, "Multiracial Churches Growing, Challenge for Clergy of Color," *AP NEWS*, 16 Jan. 2020, apnews.com/368b0e376eac72f84e1ccacaa45a1931.

53 Banks, "Multiracial Churches Growing"

54 "Multiracial Congregations Have Nearly Doubled, but They Still Lag behind the Makeup of Neighborhoods." *Media and Public Relations | Baylor University*, 20 June 2018, www.baylor.edu/mediacommunications/news.php?action=story&story=199850.

THE ACID TEST 133

the number of congregations that were exclusively one race had dropped from 50 percent to around 33 percent since 1988.

That's certainly something to raise a high five about. I am all for looking for the good in things and celebrating. As Christians, we should aim to encourage and affirm the positive and not focus on the doom and gloom. At the same time, we are called to be honest about what we are facing because it's only when we have done so that we can really start to have faith for God to make a difference. If we never really admit when things are dark, how can we expect more of God's light?

Take the example of when Moses led the people of God out of slavery in Egypt. He had a land flowing with milk and honey for them, and Moses sent twelve spies ahead to check out the situation. When the group came back, ten of them had bad news—they said that while the land was fertile, it was occupied by giants that were too much for the twelve tribes.

Only two of the advance party, Joshua and Caleb, disagreed. They didn't dispute the facts, good and bad; they just interpreted them differently. They told the people:

> *"The land we passed through and explored is exceedingly good. If the Lord is pleased with us, he will lead us into that land, a land flowing with milk and honey, and will give it to us. Only do not rebel against the Lord. And do not be afraid of the people of the land, because we will devour them. Their protection is gone, but the Lord is with us. Do not be afraid of them." (Numbers 14:7-9)*

So when it comes to our churches more closely resembling heaven, reports like the one from Baylor University are to be welcomed as a step in the right direction. However, we still have a long way to go. Just turn one of the major findings on its head: if one in five worshipers is going somewhere that is multiracial, that means that four out of five aren't. That certainly could be because of lack of choices due to population and geographic location, but these aren't the circumstances that I am referring to here.

A separate study by LifeWay Research not only found a similar multiracial worship level to the Baylor study, but it also learned that two-thirds of people felt that their church had done enough to become racially diverse. Less than half believed more needed to be done.[55]

Not only that, but one in three respondents disagreed strongly with the idea that more needed to be done. Those who identified as evangelicals were the most likely to say their church was diverse enough, while whites were least likely to say their church should become more diverse. African Americans and Hispanic Americans were more likely to say their church needed to be more diverse.[56]

Drilling down into the details, some of the ways respondents' views broke down demographically were interesting:

- Women were more likely than men to say being a minority in a congregation would make them feel uncomfortable.

- Those aged 65 and older were less likely than 18- to 24-year-olds (50 percent) to agree that churches in America are too segregated.

Ed Stetzer, the executive director of LifeWay Research, was surprised by some of the findings. "In a world where our culture is increasingly diverse, and many pastors are talking about diversity, it appears most people are happy where they are—and with whom they are," he commented. "Yet, it's hard for Christians to say they are united in Christ when they are congregating separately."[57]

Amen to that.

---

55 Bob Smietana, "Sunday Morning in America Still Segregated – and That's OK with Worshipers," *LifeWay Research*, 22 Dec. 2020, lifewayresearch.com/2015/01/15/sunday-morning-in-america-still-segregated-and-thats-ok-with-worshipers/.

56 Smietana, "Sunday Morning in America"

57 Smietana, "Sunday Morning in America"

CHOOSING YOUR FAMILY

Making a difference in the way the church looks to the rest of the world starts with a simple decision: this group of people is going to be your spiritual family, and you are going to stick with them come what may.

So many of us just cut and run at the first sign of trouble. Someone says something we don't like, whether it's the pastor or one of the ushers, and we are out the door looking for a new pew. We treat Sunday morning services the same way we do the restaurant we go to afterwards for lunch: Do we like the decor? Do we like the music? Do we like the menu? Do we like the staff? Do we feel like we are getting value for our money?

I'm reminded of the joke about the guy stranded all alone on a desert island for ten years. Just him—and no volleyball called Wilson to talk to like Tom Hanks had in *Castaway*. Finally, a passing ship sees him and sends out a rescue party.

As they are making their way back to the ship with the guy, they all look back at the island. One of the rescuers notices that there are three grass huts back on the island. He asks the rescued guy if he built them, and the man says yes.

"That one on the left," the rescued man points. "That was my house. And the one in the middle, that was my church."

"Oh," says one of the rescuers. "What about the other hut?"

"That?" the man answers. "Oh, that's the church I used to go to."

Silly, but not so far-fetched, right? If you have been around church for any length of time, you have probably met someone who moved on from somewhere else because they got upset over some small thing or another.

Now, of course, there has to be some sort of connection, some sense of belonging to a church. I'm not suggesting you go and find the most uncomfortable situation you can, just for the sake of it. Being part of a church means being with kindred spirits, but that connection is meant to be based on something deeper than just a similar taste in music or even agreement on every little point of doctrine.

We are put together in a body to learn from and to support one another, drawing from their strengths and giving of our own. That is how we "encourage one another and build each other up" (1 Thessalonians 5:11) and "stimulate one another to love and good deeds" (Hebrews 10:24).

Let's remember that church is supposed to be much more than just the place we go on Sundays. The church is not the physical building; it's the people there. It is where we, "like living stones, are being built into a spiritual house to be a holy priesthood, offering spiritual sacrifices acceptable to God through Jesus Christ" (1 Peter 5:11).

I love my earthly family. My mother has been our unofficial family historian and has traced back our roots this way and that. It has been interesting to learn about my family's past. I'm proud of uncles I have learned about who were born into the coal camps of West Virginia and through faith and hard work rose above their circumstances. One of them became the first black president of his union in New York City; another became a head postmaster. Mom started the Tucker/Dobson family reunion, on her parents' side, that brings together a hundred or more of us from across the country every year or so. It's been going on for some forty years.

Tabatha and I will always try to be there for any in our families who need us, just because they are our people. But we believe that our spiritual family is just as important. We may not share physical characteristics with others in Alive like we do with our relatives, but we share spiritual DNA and a heritage. Our earthly bloodlines may be different, but we are united by Jesus' blood that was shed on the cross for us.

Jesus loved His earthly family. When He was dying on the cross, He was still concerned enough for His mother's well-being after He was gone—widows in those days had to rely on family to care for them—that He asked one of the disciples, John, to look out for her (John 19:2-27). Yet He also made the point that the family of God was even more important. Don't miss this, because Jesus always pointed us to the kingdom perspective.

One time, early in His ministry, Mary and some of Jesus' half-siblings came to where He was teaching to try to get him to come home; they thought all this ministry stuff was getting out of hand. Jesus' response?

"Who are my mother and my brothers?" Then he looked at those seated in a circle around him and said, "Here are my mother and my brothers! Whoever does God's will is my brother and sister and mother" (Mark 3:33-35).

He wasn't dissing His own; He was just making His priorities clear. On another occasion, when Jesus was emphasizing the cost of being His disciple, He said,

"If anyone comes to me and does not hate father and mother, wife and children, brothers and sisters—yes, even their own life—such a person cannot be my disciple. And whoever does not carry their cross and follow me cannot be my disciple" (Luke 14:26-27).

The point was not literally that people had to hate their parents—just as He didn't mean for people to literally pluck out their eye if it was an avenue of temptation to sin (Matthew 5:29). That was just a common way of making a point in that time, by using hyperbole, just like we might say we could eat a horse. Not really—just a very big meal. In the same way, Jesus was emphasizing the importance of spiritual family.

Our church family should be as important to us, and we should be as committed to it as our physical family because we will be spending eternity together, brothers and sisters with our heavenly Father. Just as God chose a physical family for us to be part of, He also has a church family in mind for us: 1 Corinthians 12:18 says that He has "placed the parts in the body, every one of them, just as he wanted them to be."

For some, that's not a hard choice to make because they have never known the joys of being part of a stable family. Their only experience of family may have been when it failed—abandonment, abuse, addiction. For them, finding family in church is just great. For most of us, though, it has probably been a mixed bag—lots of good things, times, and memories, and just enough difficulties to remind us that we are all imperfect. We know that family ties are strong. That means we hang in there with each other. We forgive their strange ways. We are there for them.

I'm not saying you should turn your back on your natural family by any means, but you need to commit to the one you are adopted into as one of God's children, the church. It is going to last forever, and, even more than your earthly family, it can reflect something of heaven while you're here.

CHAPTER ELEVEN

DOING THE HARD WORK OF FORGIVENESS

As I have hinted, my wife didn't have it easy growing up. I'm not going to go into all the details here, because it's her story to tell—one day. It was hard for her being mixed, not black enough for the blacks and not white enough for the whites. Being called a "mutt" was one of the nicer things she heard. As the odd one out whichever way she turned, she'd have to fight someone on the school bus most days. It was hard living in the poor part of town, where cash was always short and many relied on the first of the month to see them through.

Then there was the loss of her daddy as a young girl. He was a Golden Gloves boxer who collapsed in the locker room after a fight one night, taken out by a brain aneurysm. That left a gap in her life and opened the door for someone who abused her in more ways than one. It was not surprising that, by the time we met when we were in school, Tabatha had been clinically depressed for ten years. Our first dates were me accompanying her to hypnotherapy and pictotherapy sessions. She smiled outwardly, but on the inside she was seriously depressed. She was heavily medicated and suicidal.

Then she met Jesus. She got filled with the Holy Spirit shortly after, and the Bible came alive. Tabatha took a hold of Proverbs 18:21 as though it had been written just for her: "The tongue has the power of life and death, and those who love it will eat its fruit." For three months, she looked herself in the bathroom mirror every morning and spoke that verse to herself as a declaration and a promise. There would be tears streaming down her face as she countered the lies she had been told all her life—that she was nothing and would never amount to anything—with God's truth.

She was not an accident. Rather, God said, "Before I formed you in the womb I knew you, before you were born I set you apart" (Jeremiah 1:5).

She was not a racial mismatch. No, she was "fearfully and wonderfully made" (Psalms 139:14).

She was not destined for a life of hopelessness. To the contrary, God said, "'For I know the plans I have for you,' declares the Lord, 'plans to prosper you and not to harm you, plans to give you hope and a future'" (Jeremiah 29:11).

There were other verses that spoke about God's goodness and healing, His freedom and restoration. Tabatha would declare them and believe them too. And you know what? Over a period of time, she felt the depression leave her. Until one day, there was no more Prozac, no more therapy—and that was almost twenty years ago.

I share all that not only to celebrate my wife's wonderful example of faith, but to illustrate that no pit is too dark that God can't lift us up out of it.

King David had a similar experience. He is believed to have written Psalm 40 about a time before he was king, when he was on the run from Saul.

He may have been anointed king by the prophet Samuel, but the chances of that ever coming about seemed remote. In verses 1-3, he wrote,

> *I waited patiently for the Lord; he turned to me and heard my cry. He lifted me out of the slimy pit, out of the mud and mire; he set my feet on a rock and gave me a firm place to stand. He put a new song in my mouth, a hymn of praise to our God. Many will see and fear the Lord and put their trust in him.*

Believing God had a brighter future for her than she had been led to expect was only part of the breakthrough for Tabatha. As well as looking ahead with confidence, she also had to look back with compassion. She had to forgive.

That meant facing the person who had been responsible for some of her deepest wounds. Humanly speaking, that was a tall order, but Tabatha knew it was the right thing to do. Because God's love had so transformed her life, she wanted everyone else to experience the same joy and freedom—even this person.

We visited him, and while part of me was mad at him for what he had done to Tabatha, more of me was just so full of admiration for her confidence and faith in facing the person who had been the cause of so much hurt. She didn't yell or cuss; she just wanted to tell him face to face that she had forgiven him for what he had done.

Her example made an impact. The person she went to said he was sorry for what he had done, though he said that he didn't remember it because he had been under the influence (which is quite possible). The story didn't end there. Later, I was able to lead this person to salvation in Jesus. On another occasion, when we were visiting, Tabatha kissed him on his forehead, blessed him, and prayed for him—what an amazing moment to witness. At one stage, we were even considering allowing this person to come and live with us and our kids, despite Tabatha's childhood experiences, because we felt God leading us that way. Looking back, this is not something we would advise anyone to do, but I share this to show how tender our hearts were in that forgiveness. While his moving in with us did not happen, there was no lingering anger or resentment on Tabatha's part. She had no unfinished business. It was all behind.

My experiences weren't as traumatic as Tabatha's, but I have had my own journey of forgiveness. Some people suffer a major wounding while others face "death by a thousand cuts," which takes its name from a gruesome kind of torture back in history. The victims were given a series of small cuts, none of which were deadly on its own but which together caused immense pain and eventually led to death.

There have been lots of people I have had to forgive, hurts I have had to let go of—like Tiffany, who was the first person to rudely awaken me to the reality of racism. There have been many others since—people who have said things or looked a certain way when I have walked into a room or a restaurant. Then, there have been those I have done my best to help as a pastor who have criticized me or complained.

I had to learn that, in ministry, you are dealing with hurting people, and hurt people hurt people—even when they don't mean to. In ministry, you are dealing with broken people, and sometimes their sharp edges will cut you as you try to help them. In ministry, you are dealing with human beings who aren't perfect—none of us are.

That includes me. I am anointed of God for an office that is holy and honorable, and God is changing me more and more into His likeness, but I am still an imperfect person (like everyone else) who is in need of a lot of grace. In fact, I came to realize that one of the reasons that I felt the kind of hurt that I did from people I was trying to help was that some of my leadership had traces of control in it, rather than complete faith in God. I have learned that people are God's responsibility, not mine. My job is to love them coming, love them going, and do all that I can to help them find God's will for their lives.

Forgiveness means that other people don't owe me an apology, either for a bad thing they may have done to me or for not acknowledging a good thing I may have done for them. No one owes me for what they did that they shouldn't have or for what they didn't do that they should have.

Forgiveness also means letting go of judgments of people. When Jesus was nailed to the cross, He prayed, "Father, forgive them, for they do not know what they are doing" (Luke 23:34). He was saying that they didn't really recognize what they were doing or how they were being used by the enemy. It's the same with people today. We are quick to think their motives for hurting or harming us in some way may be this or that, but it may not be. They could just be repeating what they learned growing up. I'm not saying their actions are any less painful, but they may not be blatantly malicious.

It has been said that holding onto unforgiveness is like drinking poison and expecting the other person to die. That's so true. Some people refuse to forgive because they feel like, by doing so, they are teaching the person or people who hurt them a lesson. Unfortunately, they end up hurting themselves instead. Not only do they continue to stew in the resentment and anger they have for what happened, they also limit God's ability to work in their lives.

Does that sound extreme? Well, remember what Jesus taught in The Lord's Prayer: "Forgive us our debts, as we also have forgiven our debtors" (Matthew 6:12). In other words, our wrongdoing will only be forgiven by God to the level we have forgiven others for the ways they have wronged us. I know I want God's forgiveness for all my sins and failures; that means I cannot hold unforgiveness toward others.

The ultimate example of forgiveness is seen at Calvary as Jesus is nailed to the cross, bloody and beaten. At the height of His pain and agony, He looks towards heaven and asks God the Father to forgive those who betrayed and bruised Him.

What an example.

FROM VICTIM TO VICTOR

I know what it's like to feel like you are starting way behind others in a race because of the history of your color. I love free stuff just like the next guy, so if someone sends me a check, I am going to deposit it—thank you very much! There even seems to be an element of justice in being given some of what was taken from your ancestors.

But as a man of faith, I believe that this line of thinking is more of a trap than a way to freedom. If unforgiveness is holding onto something with the expectation of being "repaid" somehow, then expecting reparations or restitution, could be indicative of unforgiveness.

Romans 8:12 says, "Let no debt remain outstanding, except the continuing debt to love one another, for whoever loves others has fulfilled the law." So I don't claim a debt is due. I don't believe the government owes me anything for what happened in the past. I don't believe white people owe me anything for the wrongs of their forefathers. As a Christian, I am not living my life staring in the rear-view mirror. I am looking ahead to what's coming. I am looking to God, not the government, to give me what I need.

The Bible does talk about being compensated for what was taken from you, however. Proverbs 6:31 says that when a thief is caught, "he must pay sevenfold." That sounds like a good return to me! The difference is that this comes from God, not from men.

When Jesus spoke about Satan, He called him a thief who "comes only to steal and kill and destroy" (John 10:10). Ultimately, the devil uses racism to steal from us all—black, white, and every other color. Our payback comes from God. He is the source of our increase. Scripture tells us this time and time again:

> "But remember the Lord your God, for it is he who gives you
> the ability to produce wealth, and so confirms his covenant,
> which he swore to your ancestors, as it is today."
> —Deuteronomy 8:18

*"The Lord will open the heavens, the storehouse of his bounty, to send
rain on your land in season and to bless all the work of your hands."*
—Deuteronomy 28:12

"Wealth and honor come from you."
—Chronicles 29:12

"The Lord is my shepherd, I lack nothing."
—Psalm 23:1

*"No one from the east or the west or from the desert can exalt themselves.
It is God who judges: He brings one down, he exalts another."*
—Psalm 76:6-8

Waiting on compensation from man makes me a victim, but in Jesus I am a victor. I can do all things through Christ who strengthens me (Philippians 4:13), and that has included breaking generational strongholds that have tried to hold me back and getting out of debt.

Some of our ancestors were freed from their physical chains in the nineteenth century, thankfully; but some of us are still bound by spiritual chains. Benjamin Watson puts it this way: "Living in a constant state of unforgiveness is itself a kind of bondage. When we obsess over injustice and never let it go, it controls us, and we become slaves again."[58] We need God's power to help us break out of poverty thinking, victim thinking, woe-is-me thinking, I-am-owed-something thinking.

It's time to stop blaming where you are on anyone else. It's time to take control of your life. God has a plan and purpose for you—right where you are—and it's not too late to take your first steps into that future He has in mind.

---

58 Benjamin Watson and Ken Petersen, *Under Our Skin*

I'm not saying it will all just fall into your lap. You will have to stir your-self up and cooperate with God in seeing it all come to pass. God gave the Jews the Promised Land, but they had to fight for it. As the saying goes, you have to get away from the turkeys if you want to fly with the eagles. That may mean spending less time with certain family members and friends who are like an anchor dragging on your boat when you are trying to catch the wind of God's Spirit.

Be careful about what you consume. If you want a healthy body, you need to follow a healthy diet. I found that I needed to limit what I watched and read about the ways in which black people were mistreated in the past because it often left me feeling angry and embittered. I'm not talking about ignoring the ugly things of history—and there is a place for feeling some of God's righteous anger over injustice. However, I knew I couldn't let the weight of the past keep me from rising up for my future.

And when it comes to diet, you need to balance your intake. Only watching your preferred source of news—whether that is CNN or Fox News—isn't going to help you see well. Sadly, much of the media today presents a "colored" view of the world, mixing commentary and reporting, rather than hard and clear facts.

As Christians, the same God who spoke the universe into existence lives inside of us. And with His help, we can break down racial barriers and walk in all of His precious and powerful promises. Let's start right now. Let's start by forgiving one another for the things that have been done to us, either personally or in your family's past. Seriously, right now: take a moment and begin to speak it out. Open your mouth and forgive people for slavery, for discrimination, for prejudicial remarks, for passing you up for jobs, for calling you names, for rejecting you, and abandoning you. Let's not wait another day.

We have to teach this to and model it for our kids. They are going to be hurt somewhere along the way. They need to know that "we do not wrestle against flesh and blood" (Ephesians 6:12, NKJV). We have to teach them that there is an enemy of our souls, and his name is Satan. They need to know he likes to use ignorant people to hurt us, but that we can't walk in bitterness towards people and live free at the same time. We have to truly forgive to truly live.

CHAPTER TWELVE

THE POWER OF LOVE

There is a saying in the recovery community that beating addiction is simple, but it isn't easy. You just need to stop using whatever it is that you are trying to fill that big hole inside you with. Stop drinking. Stop drugging. Stop binge-eating. Stop watching porn. Stop shopping. Whatever—just stop it. And that's true. It's simple, yes. Easy, no.

The same is true when it comes to dealing with racism. I wish I had some big secret to reveal to you at the end of this book, some sort of great revelation that would make you go, "Wow, that's so deep." But the truth is, the answer to racism really isn't very complicated. In fact, it's the same one that is true for most problems: it's love.

Some people may say that's childish naïveté. I say it's childlike hope. Jesus said, "Truly I tell you, unless you change and become like little children, you will never enter the kingdom of heaven" (Matthew 18:3).

Why do we have such a hard time putting love into practice? Well, many of us have a distorted view of what love really is. Movies and music have led us to believe that love is all about good feelings.

Now, I'm all for feeling good! As an R&B fan, I love the way Mary J. Blige puts it in her hit song, "Real Love":

> Real love, I'm searching for a real love
> Someone to set my heart free
> Real love, I'm searching for a real love.[59]

That's still my jam. After all, it doesn't get much better than when your heart feels free with someone special, right? But you know those butterfly feelings you get in your stomach the first time you meet someone? They are not always going to be there.

I hit the jackpot with Tabatha. She is beautiful, bold, brave—I could just go on and on. She inspires me to be my best self, and we make a great team. Our personalities and strengths go together well. Doing ministry with her is wonderful, but it's not all been a walk in the park, by any means.

When we first met, she was wearing someone else's engagement ring. It was at a football game at West Virginia. I was a freshman who'd been there barely a couple of weeks, and she was in her second year. She was sitting behind the group I was with in the bleachers, and I noticed how cute she was. I tried to ask her name as we passed by each other, but she just held up her hand with the ring on it, without speaking to me.

At the time, just eighteen, I wasn't looking for anything serious. In fact, I was dating around a bit. A few months after I saw Tabatha for the first time, though, I was riding in a car with a friend when I started to talk about her. "She's going to be my wife one day," I told him, "you wait and see."

---

59 Mary J. Blige, "Real Love," #3 on *What's the 411?* Uptown Records, 1992.

I have no idea where that came from, and I wasn't really walking with God at the time (just doing my Sunday repentance thing), but it turned out to be prophetic. A few months later, about a year-and-a-half after that football game, Tabatha and I met at a nightclub, which tells you something about our spiritual states. I'd heard that she had broken up with her fiancé, so I went over to introduce myself. We hit it off pretty well. The next day, I decided to forget all that wait-a-while-to-call stuff. I called and asked her if she would like to have dinner. She said yes, and that was pretty much it.

It wasn't all smooth sailing, though. As much as I loved her, I was still pretty self-focused. The first eighteen months or so of our marriage were hard, to be honest, and it was touch-and-go whether we would make it. In fact, I was thinking about divorce. Then, I got given a cake that prompted me to go to church, and everything changed as a result.

We have been together over twenty-two years now, and it all just keeps getting better. Even so, I don't feel butterflies every single day. There are times she gets on my nerves, and there are for sure times when I get on hers. However, our marriage isn't just based on our feelings for each other—good as they are most of the time. Feelings are like the weather; they change. Our marriage is based on more than that—it's based on covenant and commitment. We have made the choice that, rich or poor, ups or downs, in sickness or in health, we are together until death do us part.

This isn't some kind of life sentence. It's not a matter of "cheaper to keep her" or staying together for the sake of the kids. It's not what we "have" to do—it's what we choose to do. We have decided to spend our lives together and to love each other through every season that comes.

I love how one of our Alive members embraced this attitude for his marriage—even before his wedding day! He decided that he wasn't going to arrange one of those elaborate surprise proposals you see all over the internet these days—you know, hot air balloons and flocks of doves and orchestras, all of it caught by a video crew.

No, he decided that he was going to wait until his fiancée was having a really bad day, and then he was going to ask her to marry him. They were both professional athletes, so he knew there would come a tough training day when she was not at her best. He bought a ring and kept it tucked away.

Sure enough, the rough day came, and that was when he brought out the diamond. There was no one to capture the moment; it was just between the two of them. He told her that he loved her and that, even in the hard times, he was in it with her for the long haul. He didn't want to start out life together with everything picture-perfect, he said, because he knew that life wasn't really like that. He wanted them to begin with authenticity and a commitment to be together, to be a team, whatever came their way, no matter how tough things might get.

Now, there may have been no fireworks and frills, but for me, that was truly romantic! And this is the kind of committed, steadfast love that will overcome racism (incidentally, this is an interracial couple)!

THIS IS NOT AN OPTION

You may be thinking, *That's all very well, but romantic love doesn't have anything to do with addressing racism.* After all, when two people fall in love, there's an initial attraction that can inspire them to push through all the problems because they want to keep or rediscover what first brought them together. There isn't that positive spark toward a different group of people you might not care for—in fact, there could be sparks of a less positive kind.

That's true. We use the term "love" so loosely these days. You might say that you love your spouse, your dog, your favorite shirt, and your commute to work. The feelings you have toward each of those are probably different, though. We need more than one word to describe something that can be so varied, just as the Eskimos have fifty words for snow. Because snow is such a central part of their lives, it is important for them to be clear about exactly what kind they are referring to. The same should be true for us when it comes to love.

In Greek, the language of the New Testament, there are four words for love. There's *eros*, the tingly kind of romantic love I have been talking about. It's celebrated in Song of Solomon in no uncertain way; that book should have an R rating! But it's not limited to expressing the love between a man and a woman.

The Bible uses marriage as a picture of God's love for us. Some people see the whole of Song of Solomon as an extended metaphor of just how much God loves us (while I believe that's true, I don't think we should spiritualize it all away. That book also makes it clear that God thinks the difference between a man and a woman is something to be celebrated, and I am with Him all the way on that!).In the New Testament, we see the church referred to as the Bride of Christ. Paul uses the imagery of intimacy between a husband and wife to try to explain Jesus' great love for His people:

> *"For this reason a man will leave his father and mother and be united to his wife, and the two will become one flesh." This is a profound mystery—but I am talking about Christ and the church.* (Ephesians 5:31-32).

The Bible even uses romantic love gone wrong to give us an idea of God's love. In the book of Hosea, God tells the prophet to go marry a prostitute named Gomer. They have some kids together, and then she goes back to her old ways, leaving him as a single dad. She's out there selling herself on the streets. Talk about heartbreak.

What does God do? He tells Hosea to go after her and buy her back, to take her in and forgive her. What a powerful picture of God's redemptive love, pursuing us even when we run away from Him.

I've seen this kind of love in real life. A couple in our church came to me when the wife found that her husband had a serious porn addiction. She felt utterly betrayed, and it seemed like their marriage was over. Then, God's love broke through.

He was convicted about his sin. He repented, he went to counseling, and he did whatever he had to do to get better. She forgave him. Miraculously, as they each turned to God, He restored their marriage. At the time of writing this, they are expecting their first baby! It's a great example of how God's love can make it possible for us to forgive people who hurt us deeply in one way or another.

Then there is *storge* love. This is the kind you find in families, the kind that people are referring to when they talk about blood being thicker than water. It doesn't mean that you always get along, but it does mean that you are always there for each other, come what may, through thick and thin.

I'm reminded of one woman I know and her younger brother. Having grown up together through some hard times, they really love each other; but like many siblings, they are not afraid to let the other one know just what they think about something. Sometimes, to hear them go at it, you might get a little bit nervous; but if you were to try to step in on one side or the other, watch out! They would come together and have each other's backs before you even knew it. They can go at each other, but you'd better not try!

Next up is *phileo* love, which describes the brotherly affection you might have for a dear friend. That's why Philadelphia is known as "The City of Brotherly Love." Paul extols this kind of commitment when he writes in Romans 12:3 (TLB), "Love each other with brotherly affection and take delight in honoring each other."

However, the most important kind of love in Scripture is *agape*. When Paul writes in the famous "love passage" in 1 Corinthians 13 about how three things will remain when this world is all over—faith, hope, and love—and how "the greatest of these is love" (v. 13), he is referring to *agape*. It means benevolence, goodwill. It's about selflessness, having another's best interests at heart.

Agape love is unconditional. With the other kinds, it's easy for love to become conditional—I will be nice to you if you will be nice to me. That's why people "fall out of love," because they don't think they are getting what they deserve anymore. *Agape* says I will love you come what may, whether you "deserve" it or not.

When he talks about racial reconciliation, John Gray says it requires "a love that makes me fight for you, even though I don't see what you see. I'm talking about a love that makes me cross the bridge of understanding away from my fearful place. I'm talking about a bridge that makes me see you face to face."[60]

This is God's love for us, one that reaches out. It's just as well, too, because if He withheld His love from us until we deserved it, we would all still be waiting. The good news of the gospel is that "God demonstrates his own love for us in this: While we were still sinners, Christ died for us" (Romans 5:8). As someone has said, the highest expression of God's love for us—His death and resurrection—came at our lowest point. That worst, most shameful event or episode from your past? Covered by Jesus' love and blood, completely.

How is this possible? Love isn't just something God does. It is His essence. It is Who He is. 1 John 4:16 says, "God *is* love. Whoever lives in love lives in God, and God in them" (emphasis added).

As children of God, this is the kind of love that we are called to have for other people. It is a love that is not based on personal preferences, but on

---

60 "Pastor John Gray: The Bridge Supersoul Sessions," *YouTube*, 10 May 2017, www.youtube.com/watch?v=7Rk5WFj5rEQ.

the fact that other people are made in the image of God. It is a love that doesn't change like the tides or the blowing of the wind.

This isn't a wimpy, weak kind of love. It's actually the strongest force in the universe. It is what propelled Jesus to Calvary, where He broke the power of sin and death once and for all. And, though it may seem like a tall order, it isn't an option for us. It's a command.

One day, one of the Jewish legal experts asked Jesus which of the Ten Commandments was the most important. Bear in mind that, by this stage, the religious leaders had expanded on those ten rules with a whole lot of other right and wrong ways of doing things, so that there were around six hundred written and oral laws that the Jews were supposed to follow concerning every area of life.

Jesus' answer? He replied,

"'Love the Lord your God with all your heart and with all your soul and with all your mind.' This is the first and greatest commandment. And the second is like it: 'Love your neighbor as yourself.' All the Law and the Prophets hang on these two commandments" (Matthew 22:37-38).

Jesus gave the same answer when, on another occasion, someone asked Him how they could inherit eternal life. Then they asked Jesus who was their neighbor. Jesus' response was to tell the famous story of the Good Samaritan. When a man was beaten and robbed and left for dead, it wasn't one of the Jewish religious leaders that came to his aid. It was a Samaritan, one of a group of people despised by the Jews for their history and their ways. One commentary notes:

There are countless modern parallels to the Jewish-Samaritan enmity—indeed, wherever peoples are divided by racial and ethnic barriers It is not the person from the radically different culture on the other side of the world that is hardest to love, but the nearby neighbor whose skin color, language, rituals, values, ancestry, history, and customs are different from one's own.[61]

Jesus' "love" command wasn't just to those who may have been trying to trip Him up with a clever question. It was also to those who loved Him. At the Last Supper, He told His disciples, "A new command I give you: Love one another. As I have loved you, so you must love one another. By this everyone will know that you are my disciples, if you love one another" (John 13:34-35).

Notice that He didn't tell them to try to get along if they could. It wasn't a suggestion or a wish-list item. He directed them to love one another. "Do it," He said. Now, God doesn't tell us to do things that are impossible—with His help. Why was this instruction so important to Him? Because He also told them that others would know they were His followers by the way they treated each other—not by the miracles they performed or the Bible verses they could quote.

I believe that's where we are as the church today. We have an amazing opportunity to demonstrate that we are God's children—not by how much we know, not by how cool we are, but by how we love one another—regardless of the color of our skin. In a world of increasing tribalism, our diversity is a bright light.

FORGIVENESS AND REPENTANCE

So my answer to racism—love—may be simple, but it isn't easy. What might real love look like in everyday life as we try to become a church that looks more like heaven? It will involve two particular expressions of God's love—repentance and forgiveness. As Miles McPherson observes, "Everyone is affected by racism. Nearly every American has been a victim or a perpetrator of racism, and most have been both."[62]

---

61 "Hatred between Jews and Samaritans," *The Word in Life Study Bible, Bible.org,* bible.org/illustration/hatred-between-jews-and-samaritans.

62 Miles McPherson, *The Third Option*

Both repentance and forgiveness are costly. True repentance is more than just saying sorry; it involves doing things differently from now on. True forgiveness involves letting go of the need for revenge or recompense, no matter how unfairly you have been treated. Both repentance and forgiveness are lifestyles, not occasional acts. They are a call to ongoing, repetitive unity in the body of Christ.

When I try to picture this in action, it seems like 1 Corinthians 13:4-8 brought to life. We all know these verses well. They are a favorite at weddings; I have heard them read at many of the ceremonies I have officiated through the years:

> *Love is patient, love is kind. It does not envy, it does not boast, it is not proud. It does not dishonor others, it is not self-seeking, it is not easily angered, it keeps no record of wrongs. Love does not delight in evil but rejoices with the truth. It always protects, always trusts, always hopes, always perseveres. Love never fails.*

Let's break that down when it comes to racism.

LOVE IS PATIENT

We know that this isn't going to be an overnight fix. It will take time to understand each other better. We are committed to the long haul. We also know this isn't going to be easy: older Bible translations talk about "long-suffering" instead of patience. There is going to be some pain involved.

We live in such an instant world these days that we have forgotten how to wait for anything. We get frustrated when the stoplight doesn't turn green straight away or if that webpage doesn't load immediately. We want things to happen right now, but sometimes change takes time.

Some people like big events because they get a sense of satisfaction from being part of something. You go and walk in a protest march and feel like you have done your part. I'm not saying those kind of actions are wrong, but that's having gone and shown the world how you feel about something with a group of others. What are you doing day by day, in your own small corner, to be part of the change you made a noise about?

Benjamin Watson puts it this way:

> *Often when people reach a hand across the racial aisle, it's a gesture that serves to make themselves feel good, rather than to effect real change. Other times when we do a good thing, it can be for show— something we do only because it looks good to others. We didn't accomplish anything by creating false and sentimental kids-hugging-cops pictures. These "works" lack integrity and truth.*
>
> *No, any meaningful change we might pursue requires a willingness to engage personally, over time, getting our hands dirty in the mess of it all. This isn't a one-time appearance. It's an ongoing involvement.*[63]

How to do that? One thing he suggests is attending a racially diverse church. If you're already planted in a church, you can be part of this movement by bringing people to your church home who don't necessarily look like you and making sure they feel welcomed and loved. I know this isn't an option for everyone, considering geographical location and the population of any given place, but if it is available to you, take this step. It's all about building relationships with people outside of your culture in the context of spiritual unity. It's so rich when we operate and walk out our lives in this kingdom perspective.

LOVE IS KIND

We are tender-hearted to one another. When there are misunderstandings, we assume the best. We go out of our way to be nice. When we come across people who are racist, we aim to love the hell out of them (literally!).

---

63 Benjamin Watson and Ken Petersen, *Under Our Skin*

LOVE DOES NOT ENVY

Jealousy feeds off a sense of injustice that someone else has gotten more than their fair share. We choose to trust that God has no favorites and we don't allow ourselves to get resentful about others' success or apparent privilege. We know that God is our provider.

LOVE DOES NOT BOAST, IT IS NOT PROUD

We don't claim to be better than anyone else, so we celebrate our heritage and history without putting someone else's down. We value the good things we can see in others' backgrounds. We don't do cultural appropriation; we do cultural appreciation.

LOVE DOES NOT DISHONOR OTHERS, IT IS NOT SELF-SEEKING

We are sensitive to the ways we might inadvertently offend someone by saying something that carries a weight or a context of which we are not aware. If in doubt, we seek clarity. If we make a mistake and hurt someone, we apologize. Our emphasis is not so much on putting others right where they may be wrong but identifying and dealing with our own blindspots and prejudices. As Frances of Assisi prayed, "Grant that I may not so much seek to be consoled as to console, to be understood, as to understand."[64]

LOVE IS NOT EASILY ANGERED

We recognize that, even with their best efforts, people are going to make mistakes. There will be misunderstandings and disappointments. When that happens, we choose to respond gracefully and graciously. We address things, but we do so lovingly. And we forgive.

---

64 "The Peace Prayer Of St. Francis," *St. Anthony Messenger*, vol. 124, no. 4 (Franciscan Media, LLC: Sept. 2016) 57.

LOVE KEEPS NO RECORD OF WRONGS

We don't allow ourselves to be held captive by history. We don't ignore it, because there are lessons for us to learn. But we don't hold yesterday over someone's head as an unforgivable sin. We let it go.

The rearview mirror in your car is smaller than the windshield for a good reason: you need to spend more time looking forward than looking behind, otherwise you are going to crash. If we spend too much time looking at the past, we are not going to see our future.

LOVE DOES NOT DELIGHT IN EVIL BUT REJOICES WITH THE TRUTH

The focus of our lives together is not on what's wrong and needs to be fixed; instead, it is on the goodness and greatness of God. We are united more by what—Whom—we are for than what we are against. We concentrate on proclaiming and demonstrating the love of God.

LOVE ALWAYS PROTECTS

We don't ignore injustice when we see it. We speak up and we speak out about wrongdoing, and we work to make things better. We try to do so without being becoming angry at individuals; sadly, it seems to me that some people who are all about "justice" end up being bitter. We remember that, ultimately, this is a spiritual battle.

Being the kind of peacemakers Jesus talked about in the Sermon on the Mount doesn't mean being a doormat. Peace isn't the absence of conflict; it's the presence of God's Spirit. Peacemakers express God's righteous anger in a controlled way. Look at how Jesus cleared the temple of the moneychangers who were taking advantage of people.

LOVE ALWAYS TRUSTS, IT ALWAYS HOPES, IT ALWAYS PERSEVERES

We don't ignore the bad news, but we choose to trust the small print of the Bible more than today's headlines. When there is another racial blowup somewhere, we acknowledge it and discuss it, but we don't let ourselves get discouraged. We trust that love will win out in the end.

LOVE NEVER FAILS

As fallen human beings, we are never going to get it all right all the time. We will make mistakes, we will misunderstand. If we keep getting up every time we stumble, we haven't failed; we've just fallen for a moment. Failure is only final when you give up and don't get up again.

Inventor Thomas Edison was once asked what it was like to have failed a thousand times before he successfully created the first light bulb. He said that he hadn't failed a thousand times—rather, the light bulb had been an invention with a thousand steps. That's the kind of attitude that we need to have.

One of the reasons love is the key is that it is the ultimate weedkiller for the roots of racism, which is fear—fear of those who are different. However, 1 John 4:18 declares, "There is no fear in love. But perfect love drives out fear, because fear has to do with punishment. The one who fears is not made perfect in love." The Apostle John goes on to deliver a serious warning to anyone who claims to love God but harbors racial division somewhere in their heart:

> *Whoever claims to love God yet hates a brother or sister is a liar. For whoever does not love their brother and sister, whom they have seen, cannot love God, whom they have not seen. And he has given us this command: Anyone who loves God must also love their brother and sister (1 John 4:20-21).*

How do we do that? Welcome and intentionally bring people from different backgrounds and cultures into your home. This is much easier to do in the context of your local church if you attend one that is racially diverse, because hospitality is a given in the body of Christ. I believe that if we will lock arms and walk together in the kind of supernatural love John speaks of, the kind that is only possible with God's Spirit living inside us, we can be part of bringing about racial harmony, healing, and unity. I am not being all pie-in-the-sky about this, because we have seen a glimpse of this before.

At our church, we believe that the Holy Spirit is alive and well and living in us! He continues to perform the kind of miracles we read Jesus did in the Bible. We're part of the movement born out of the famous Azusa Street Revival in 1906.

At that time, "[S]outhern churches were completely separated by race; Christianity had divided along the color line."[65] Then William J. Seymour, a black pastor, began to hold services in Los Angeles, California, that attracted blacks, whites, Asians, and Mexicans. Seymour had been allowed to attend a white Pentecostal leader's Bible school on the condition he sat outside a partly-ajar door.

Daniel Norris, an evangelist, says that the Azusa Street movement could in many ways "be considered the first civil rights movement of the 1900s, and it started in a multiracial prayer meeting!"[66] He observes:

> It was written that, "The 'color line' was washed away in the blood." Another declared "the 'Azusa' work had rediscovered the blood of Christ to the church it was a sort of 'first love' of the early church returned. The baptism as we received it in the beginning did not allow us to think, speak or hear evil of any man."

65 "A Glimpse of the Kingdom of Heaven: The Azusa Street Revival," *This Far By Faith: African-American Spiritual Journeys*, PBS, https://www.pbs.org/thisfarbyfaith/journey_3/p_9.html.

66 Daniel K. Norris, "How Azusa Street Exposed-and Overturned-Racism in the Church." *Charisma News*, 11 Oct. 2016, www.charismanews.com/opinion/from-the-frontlines/60462-how-azusa-street-exposed-mdash-and-overturned-mdash-racism-in-the-church.

How had Azusa accomplished what so few could have even imagined at that time? Simple, at the heart of revival is a message of reconciliation—first to God and, as a consequence, to one another.[67]

The Azusa Street Revival spread across the nation and around the world, but sadly would split "along theological and racial lines."[68] For his part, "Seymour came to believe that blacks and whites worshiping together was a surer sign of God's blessing and the Spirit's healing presence than speaking in tongues. The fact that the church had nationally split along racial lines meant that the charismatic ideal of cooperation with the Spirit had been foiled by the forces of racism."[69]

A century after the Azusa Street Revival, it's time to rediscover its full impact—the power of the Holy Spirit demonstrated not only in physical signs and wonders but in the supernatural healing of our racial divide. I feel like God wants to do the same and more in this generation—a greater revival with greater impact, especially as it relates to healing our racial divide.

Many times, when it comes to dealing with racism, we look for some sort of organization to do the job. I believe that the church has the biggest part to play. When I say the church, I am not talking about an institution, the church with a capital C. I am referring to the church as the body of Christ, made up of every single born-again believer who calls on the name of Jesus.

We each have a role to play, and the fact that you have invested your time in reading this book tells me that God has hand-selected you. Jesus said that "many are called, but few are chosen" (Matthew 22:14, NKJV). My hope in writing this book has been to help equip those who respond to His invitation, as you have done. As we end this journey together, first, let

---

67 Norris, "How Azusa Street"
68 "A Glimpse of the Kingdom"
69 "A Glimpse of the Kingdom"

me thank you for being part of the solution. Thank you for loving Jesus and for loving His people and for loving His world.

Now is the time to let our light shine. It's dark, but that is precisely when the light shines brightest. We face a big problem, but we have the answer, and His name is Jesus. Through Him, we can be part of bringing a little bit of heaven to earth.

None of us can change the whole world, but we can change our corner of it. Start small. If you're aware of ways in the past that you have been unloving to someone of another color, reach out and apologize. Stretch out across the racial divide. Open your refrigerator—and your heart.

Remember, when God looks at us, He doesn't see lots of different races. He sees one race—the human race, as it is in heaven.

FIVE STONES FOR YOUR SLINGSHOT

Love does something. It is an action, but it doesn't have to be big. Here are five ideas to get you going. Think of them like the small stones David gathered up when he, armed only with a slingshot, went to confront Goliath the giant. You can come at the giant of racism with these five rocks:

Say your prayers. *Well, of course,* you may be thinking. But, seriously, pray. Don't just talk about it. Start by asking that God would show you any prejudice that may be lodged in a corner of your heart and uproot it. Having begun with personal change, then pray that God may change others' hearts too. Be encouraged by the prophet Elijah: when he prayed, a three-year drought came to an end (1 Kings 18). Prayer is powerful!

Use your ears. I've written about how important empathy is; well, the first step in being empathetic is listening well, really trying to hear and see things from someone else's point of view. Be a good listener. Be willing to hear from those who know more about the issue than you do or who maybe experience it differently than you. Commit to being uncomfortable, and avoid the temptation to argue when you disagree with someone. You don't have to agree with everything that is said; take the meat and leave the bones. There is a time for dialogue, but giving your opinions too quickly tells the other person you haven't really listened to them.

Exercise your platform. You may not have a gazillion followers on social media. You may not even have a social media profile at all. But you do have a presence in other people's lives that can be a place of influence—as a parent, relative, neighbor, work colleague, or friend. That may require you to speak up when someone says something racist, even though doing so will be awkward or uncomfortable. You don't need to lecture, but you can share with them your heart for racial reconciliation and ask them for their thoughts and experiences. You could invite others to wrestle with the issue of racism by sharing about this book on Facebook or Instagram; post the cover, and share how reading it has informed or inspired you.

Make your contribution. Real involvement costs something. It could be your time, your money—even your reputation, if some people don't agree with you. Sign meaningful petitions, contact your legislators to urge them to action, participate in some sort of public expression of anti-racism. Vote for the leaders you believe can help bring about positive change. Send money to organizations that are working to dismantle racism and helping those most affected by it. Perhaps you might want to start a small group that is intentionally diverse, to begin talking and praying about this issue together. Find some way to introduce your children to other cultures and colors. Consider moving to a more diverse community or neighborhood.

Drop your rocks. *What?* you may be thinking. *First you tell me to pick up stones, and now you are telling me to put them down?* The point is, remember that we don't throw things at people. Like David, we take aim at the root of the problem, the enemy of God. It's very easy—appropriate, even—to get fired up about terrible injustice like racism. You can allow yourself to get angry. God certainly does! Proverbs 6:16-19 says,

There are six things the Lord hates, seven that are detestable to him:
haughty eyes, a lying tongue, hands that shed innocent blood, a heart
that devises wicked schemes, feet that are quick to rush into evil, a
false witness who pours out lies and a person who stirs up conflict in
the community.

There are things He is seriously not okay with. However, through Paul, He also tells us, "In your anger do not sin: Do not let the sun go down while you are still angry" (Ephesians 4:26). Like the mob that wanted to stone the woman who was caught in adultery and brought to Jesus (John 8:1-11), we need to drop our stones and walk away. Forgiveness and repentance are essential. We don't solve hatred with hate. Jesus said, "Blessed are the peacemakers" (Matthew 5:9).

If ever you are in Gainesville or Orlando, I'd love for you join us at Alive Church, to experience how we try to resemble heaven together. To find out more about our ministries, our locations, and service times, go to www.myalivechurch.org.

If you would like to keep up with me personally as I continue to pray, preach, and write about a multiracial church that resembles heaven, you can do so on Instagram (@KenClaytor), Facebook (@PastorKenClaytor) and YouTube (@AliveChurch).

God bless you!